T.L.C.

TENDER LOVING COVERS

by Toni Phillips and Juanita Simonich

We should have old memories and a young outlook.

POSSIBILITIES®

8970 E. HAMPDEN AVE. DENVER, CO 80231
(303) 740-6206   FAX (303) 220-7424

►. A SPECIAL THANK YOU TO: .◄

Juanita's husband, Dennis, for being our biggest fan, bringing us lunch, doing the dishes, proofreading, and putting up with long hours without complaint.

Our children, Katie Phillips, Michael Phillips, Luke Simonich, and Marie Simonich for enthusiasm, suggestions, help, and getting by on minimal mothering during the writing of the book.

Our mothers, Ann Schultes and Bette St. Vrain for believing in us and inspiring us to follow our dreams. Thanks to Toni's mother and Aunt Jeanne Young for picking up the slack and providing the time to do the project. To all three, for sewing bindings, buttons, and other detail work.

Our students, friends and shop customers for their enthusiasm and encouragement along the way. We especially appreciate your admiration of our quilts.

Katie Hinga, Rita Balzer, and Mary Beth Church for testing patterns.

Bev McFarland, for allowing us to photograph in her beautiful home.

Laura Asbell, our partner in Fabric Expressions, for support in this project.

Jewell Patterson for introducing Toni to quilting.

Edith Niblo, although she is gone, for teaching Juanita design, color, drawing and a love for the process.

■

CREDITS

Executive Editors - Nancy Smith & Lynda Milligan
Senior Editor - Sharon Holmes
Illustration - Marilyn Robinson
Electronic Illustration - Sharon Holmes
Photography - Brian Birlauf
Setups - Helen Hall

TABLE OF CONTENTS

PREFACE

The concept for these quilts grew out of a perceived need for children's quilt designs. As the quilts progressed, it became apparent they were to be as meaningful to the maker as they would be for the recipient, linking our generation with our children's. They are truly *Tender Loving Covers*.

As we planned and stitched, the quilts sparked childhood memories. We grew up in two entirely different areas. Juanita grew up on a farm on the plains of northeastern Montana, and Toni was raised in New York City and Houston, Texas. Many hours were spent reminiscing about the past...one-room schoolhouses, rodeos, farm life, the opening of NASA in Houston, going to a circus, visiting the zoo, and family Christmas traditions...finding out that in spite of different backgrounds, we had much in common. In the end, we not only created a book but also a friendship.

We hope these quilts generate the same tender loving feelings for you as they have for us.

Happy Stitching,

Toni & Juanita

INTRODUCTION

The first quilt completed in this series was *Trip to the Zoo*. Originally it was designed for manufacture by our pattern company, *Fabric Expressions*, but while working on it and discussing themes for other children's quilts, our ideas exploded, and we began to think about a book.

Trip to the Zoo and *E-I-E-I-O* were designed using templates. As sewing progressed, we started looking for an easier, faster way to put these pieced picture quilts together. Necessity is the mother of invention, so we expanded the idea of the pressed triangle corner we had used on a snowball block. Soon forty-five degree angles appeared everywhere. The Fast Forty-Five technique emerged. Most of the templates on the first two quilts were eliminated, and we designed the remaining quilts without templates.

Because each block is different, layered cutting techniques do not apply, but the square and rectangular pieces are easily and accurately cut with the rotary cutter. If a quilt were made repeating one of the blocks, pieces could be layer-cut. Once the cutting is complete, the blocks sew together quickly. It is exciting to watch each design evolve.

Please read the entire *General Directions* section before cutting. Save time and avoid problems by using the spray starch/freezer paper applique method, the Fast Forty-Five piecing technique, cardboard templates for smooth circles, and quick freezer paper templates for stitching loose inserts. One of our intentions in writing this book was to offer hints and tips for successful quiltmaking, so don't miss out!

Remember that you are making picture quilts, not speed quilts, so enjoy the process. You will become addicted. Sewing these quilts is never tedious or boring. They will bring back and create memories.

GENERAL DIRECTIONS

Please read the entire General Directions section before you begin.

■ AUDITIONING & PREPARING FABRIC ■

PREWASHING FABRIC

Prewashing 100% cotton fabrics is usually recommended to minimize shrinkage and color bleeding. We, however, chose to take advantage of the slight shrinkage that occurs when today's cottons are washed for the first time. The batting we used was also cotton (not prewashed), so when the quilts were washed after they were finished, the quilting stitches sank down into the fabric, emphasizing the quilting designs. However, before piecing the quilts, fabrics should be checked to make sure that the dye does not run. This can be done by soaking a sample of the fabric in hot, soapy water and squeezing it between layers of white fabric. If you can see no traces of dye, it should be safe to make the quilt without prewashing.

AUDITIONING FABRIC FOR YOUR STASH

Gathering fabrics for *Tender Loving Covers* is as much fun as sewing them into the quilts. Perhaps the most significant time put into a quilt is the time spent picking and choosing fabrics. A willingness to put aside a fabric you have chosen may make the difference between a good palette and a great palette. This process can be called "auditioning" your fabrics.

Before the designs for these quilts were complete, we began to gather a "stash" that looked good together. Setting up guidelines and parameters helps in narrowing choices and selecting fabrics. Two of the *Tender Loving Covers* stretched the parameters we set for ourselves. The themes in *Shoot for the Stars* and *Reading 'Riting, and Recess* seemed to dictate a slightly different look. We continued to use the guidelines but pushed the boundaries.

Listed below are the guidelines set for these quilts. If you want a similar "look", keep the following suggestions in mind as you make selections.
- Tan or ivory background fabric
- A variety of plaids, checks, homespuns in different sizes
- Many "solid" prints
- Grayed intensity and dark values
- No calicos or flowery prints
- No fabrics with white backgrounds

Your own guidelines for choosing fabrics are also valid. You might want to use only clear, intense colors with contemporary designs and white backgrounds, or you might choose primary colors in different values. These color choices can make an exciting quilt, but it will have a completely different look from the ones pictured in this book.

When doing the final audition for a specific quilt, it may be necessary to put aside a fabric for another project. **The color or print you choose is not as important as the one you choose to put next to it.**

■

NOTE: Yardage in this book is based on 44″ to 45″ wide 100% cotton fabric.

Eighth to quarter yard cuts of fabric are sufficient for most block piecing other than backgrounds. Several pieces from your stash will be needed to complete each quilt.

■ TOOLS & EQUIPMENT ■

FOR PIECING
Sewing machine
Fabric scissors
Rotary cutter
Rotary ruler - 24″ long
Rotary ruler - 6″ or 8″ square with diagonal and
    quarter-inch markings
Rotary cutting mat
Template plastic - small sheet
Thread

FOR APPLIQUE
Freezer paper
Heavy-duty aerosol spray starch
Inexpensive watercolor paintbrush
Gray and natural machine embroidery thread for
    hand applique
Applique needles or sharps

Marking pencil
Paper scissors
Fabric scissors with a sharp point for clipping and
    trimming
Cardboard for making circles

FOR MACHINE QUILTING
Safety pins for pin-basting
Monofilament thread, clear and smoke
Cotton or poly-cotton thread to match backing (for
    the bobbin)
Metallic thread & topstitching needle, optional
Walking foot for the sewing machine
Darning foot for the sewing machine
Continuous quilting stencils for borders and sashing
"Bicycle" clips
Rubber fingers
8-10 large binder clips

■ ROTARY CUTTING ■

It is best to use a rotary cutter to cut all of the pieces for these quilts except the applique shapes and the loose inserts. Some extra fabric is used, but the speed and accuracy compensates for the loss.

The block pieces are rectangles and squares. Cut on the straight grain, either parallel or at right angles to the selvage. For uneven plaids, stripes, or directional fabrics, cut following the design in the fabric. The 6″ or 8″ square rotary ruler is convenient for use in cutting the smaller squares and rectangles.

To square up fabric for cutting strips, bindings, and sashings, fold the fabric lengthwise, matching selvages and checking that the fabric lays flat. If you are using unwashed fabric, usually you will not need to refold. Lay folded fabric approximately 5″ from the left edge of the mat, matching the fold to the bottom line of the cutting mat. Match one of the cross-markings on the 24″ ruler with the fold. The ruler should overlap the left raw edge of the fabric by ½″. Rotary cut, forming an accurate right angle. Without disturbing the fabric, begin cutting strips from the freshly cut edge. For the quilts in this book, it works well to cut a strip of fabric the width of the widest rectangle or square, cut the largest piece from the strip first, then cut smaller pieces from the rest of the strip.

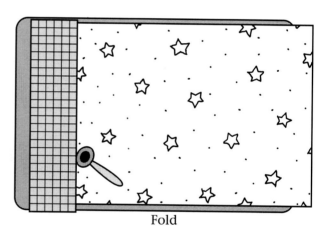
Fold

Cut borders on the lengthwise grain unless instructed otherwise; our yardage allows for this extra fabric. Lengthwise grain fabric can be folded for cutting with rotary tools also; simply make the folds at right angles to the selvage.

■ FAST FORTY-FIVES ■

Most of the *Tender Loving Covers* block designs have 45° angles. Using the Fast Forty-Five method is quick, easy, and accurate. Some fabric will be sacrificed for speed and accuracy.

Every piece, except loose inserts, is numbered and listed by fabric. **Any piece containing a letter is a Fast Forty-Five.** For example, in the following diagram, a, b, c, and d are all Fast Forty-Fives that belong to piece #1. They are identified as 1a, 1b, 1c, and 1d in the cutting charts.

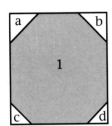

Pig body/pink
Piece	Size
1	6″ x 7″

Background/tan
Piece	Size
1a, 1b	2″ x 2″
1c, 1d	1½″ x 1½″

A Fast Forty-Five is a square that will be pressed and sewn to another piece, then opened to make a triangle. To complete the block above, cut piece #1 from pink fabric. From the tan background fabric, cut two 2″ x 2″ squares for pieces 1a and 1b, and two squares 1½″ x 1½″ for pieces 1c and 1d. Press the Fast Forty-Five squares 1a, 1b, 1c, and 1d **wrong sides** together carefully along the diagonal.

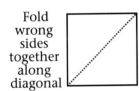

Lay #1 right side up. Place folded #1a on the correct corner of #1, matching raw edges.

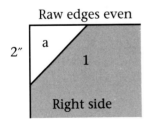

Open #1a along the pressed fold, pin, and sew one or two threads outside the diagonal fold line. This compensates for the bulk of the seam allowance.

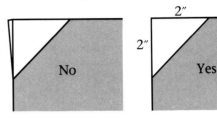

Fold back and check the accuracy of the corner by making sure the Fast Forty-Five matches the edges of the foundation piece.

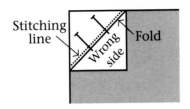

Cut away the two underneath layers, leaving a ¼″ seam allowance.

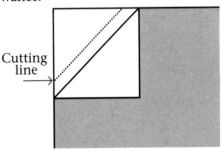

Continue until all Fast Forty-Fives are attached to piece #1.

▪ USING THE PATTERNS ▪

The speed in construction of these blocks is somewhere between fast, rotary-cut, strip piecing and traditional patchwork piecing. The **Fast Forty-Five** allows individual picture blocks to be made in minimal time. The spray starch method of applique simplifies the applique process, making diversity of shape possible, which in turn adds charm to the quilts.

Every square or rectangular cutting measurement includes a ¼″ seam allowance. Most of the quilts require no patchwork templates, although a few are necessary for the *E-I-E-I-O* and *Trip to the Zoo* quilts. **Patterns for making patchwork templates include seam allowances. Patterns for inserts and appliques <u>do not</u> include seam allowances. Seam allowances are added to inserts and appliques <u>after</u> fusing freezer paper (see Loose Inserts section and Applique section).**

SEWING

The single most important technique to master is sewing an accurate ¼″ seam. There are several different ways to achieve a ¼″ seam allowance. The needle on certain machines can be moved to the right or left. Some quilters use a piece of tape on their needle plate to mark an accurate ¼″. There may be a ¼″ presser foot available for your machine. The fabric edge can be aligned with a notch or a line marked on the foot.

To check the accuracy of your ¼″ seams, carefully cut five 1½″ strips of fabric about 6″ long with a rotary cutter. Sew all of the strips together using a ¼″ seam allowance. Press all the seams in one direction. Measure the width of the finished piece in several places. The width should be 5½″. If the piece matches that measurement, your seam is an accurate ¼″. If it is over or under, you will need to adjust the width of your seam. Sew another set of strips and remeasure.

Because the blocks have many seams, it is imperative for units to fit together exactly. Check unit sizes as you sew, and be willing to use your ripper to "unsew". Most seams are short, and immediate correction of an error is well worth the effort as it will avoid frustration later. If a unit must be stretched to fit another unit, look for the sewing error and correct it.

Stitch pieces and units right sides together unless otherwise noted.

PATTERN PIECE NUMBERS

Every pattern piece of every block has its own number except loose inserts, which are named. Generally, pieces are sewn numerically. Often a unit of pieces is stitched, then attached to another unit. Units are clearly illustrated in the pull-away block drawings.

A ★ indicates the seam in which an insert is stitched. For example, the prairie point face insert is sewn between unit 1-2 and unit 3-4. Unit 5 is completed and sewn to #6, then the wing is stitched between #3 and #6.

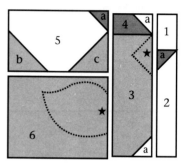

CUTTING

Do all cutting of the squares and rectangles with a rotary cutter and appropriate rulers. A 6″ or 8″ square with a diagonal line and quarter-inch markings is handy.

Shading on the illustration does not indicate individual fabrics. Shadings merely identify the dominant shapes. Fabrics are listed in the cutting chart. To "see" the fabrics, study the full-color photographs.

All of the pieces from one fabric in a block are listed separately by **description** (Car body/green stripe), by **piece number** (1, 13), and by **size** (3″ x 1½″) as shown below. The first measurement indicates crosswise grain, and the second measurement indicates lengthwise grain. If the fabric does not have a "direction", rectangles can be cut on the crosswise grain **or** the lengthwise grain; however, if the fabric has a "direction" (stripes, plaids, up-to-down prints etc.), the pieces should be cut with the first measurement lined up with the crosswise grain of the fabric.

For example, from the green stripe fabric for the car, cut #1 and #13, lining up the 3″ side on the crosswise grain. Then cut #2, lining up the 1½″ side on the crosswise grain.

Car Body/green stripe

Piece	Size
1, 13	3″ x 1½″
2	1½″ x 3″

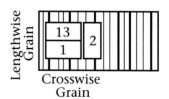

Do not cut plaids, stripes, or checks in multiple layers. Use the clear ruler to line up the plaid, stripe or check so it will appear straight on the quilt. See last paragraph of rotary cutting section for cutting tips.

To cut templates for *E-I-E-I-O* and *Trip to the Zoo*, trace the pattern accurately on plastic. Cut out the templates and trace around them **face down** on the **wrong** side of the fabric. If the pattern calls for one reversed, trace around the template **face up**. Quarter inch seam allowances are marked on the patterns. Patchwork pieces that have patterns given for making templates are marked on the block diagram with a T (11T, 12T, etc.).

After cutting, lay out the block next to your machine. You may want to pick up all of the **Fast Forty-Fives** and press them. Then lay them on the corner of the piece to which they will be stitched. An iron and ironing board within reach makes sewing easier as each seam needs to be pressed before another is sewn over it.

After one block is cut, begin to sew with pieces #1 and #2 (or #1 and #1a), following the block illustration carefully. Pick up the pieces, sew them, press, lay the new unit down in its place, and continue until the block is complete.

■ PRESSING ■

The method used to press your work will significantly affect the finished project. "Press" the seams on the back with a gentle motion, watching that every seamline is pressed flat. Use the tip of your iron on the top side of the quilt to press out any tucks along seamlines.

Do not use a back and forth motion. This will cause both appliqued and pieced blocks to pull out of shape. **Do not** finger-press, as finger-pressing causes the same problem. **This is especially true for Fast Forty-Fives.**

PRESSING PIECED UNITS

Seams in quilts are always pressed together in one direction, **not open**, for two reasons. First, the seams are stronger and won't look pulled apart. Second, ditch quilting is done on the side of the seam away from the seam allowance, making the quilting easier and nearly invisible. Pressing seams carefully is essential. Units will fit together much easier if each seam is pressed before the next seam is sewn over it.

Before pressing, consider the direction to lay the seam. Some general rules apply. Usually, it is best to press the seam toward the darker fabric; however, when sewing a pieced block to a solid piece of fabric such as a sashing strip or border, press the seams toward the fabric that is not pieced. When two seams meet, they should be pressed in opposite directions so they "butt" up to one another when stitched together.

PRESSING APPLIQUED WORK

To press an applique, use a small terry cloth towel on the ironing board. Place the applique face down and press from the back of the block so the applique will not flatten completely. Again, a gentle up-and-down motion is preferred. **Do not** "iron" back and forth as the applique will pull out of shape. The tip of your iron can smooth seams. If a flat, crisp look is desired, do not use the towel and press a second time from the front.

PRESSING LAMÉ

If you use lamé in *Shoot for the Stars*, press with a **warm** iron on the back side of the fabric. Because lamé is heat sensitive, it stretches and curls easily, so test a sample before pressing the block. Follow any directions that come with the lamé.

▪ LOOSE INSERTS ▪

Part of the charm of the *Tender Loving Covers* is the loose inserts. Little girls and boys love to open the barn doors, peek inside the school bus and feel the piggy's tail. These 3-D inserts are easy to make and quite sturdy, as they are first sewn into the seam and later machine quilted "in the ditch" to make them more durable. The quilts with the loose pieces are especially delightful when used as wallhangings.

Caution: Should you want to make these quilts for children under three years of age, for the child's safety, you should applique the ears, eyes, doors, and so on. Do not use buttons for eyes. Do not use monofilament thread for infants' quilts.

MAKING THE INSERT

Patterns for inserted pieces are not numbered, but are identified by name. These patterns **do not** include seam allowances. To make a template, trace the pattern onto the shiny side of freezer paper. Freezer paper is transparent enough to trace directly from the book. Cut out the freezer paper shape on the pattern line.

Choose an appropriate fabric. You will need two pieces at least one inch larger than the freezer paper template. Place the fabric pieces on top of each other with **right** sides together. If you want batting in the insert, lay a piece of it **under**, not between, the two layers of fabric.

Lay the freezer paper template, shiny side down, on the layered fabric, making sure that there is at least ¼" of fabric all around. Iron the freezer paper onto the fabric.

Using a sewing machine, stitch along the edge of the freezer paper, following the shape accurately. If using batting, sew a few thread widths outside of the freezer paper template to compensate for the space needed to accommodate the batting. Otherwise the pieces will end up being too small. Each piece will have at least one side open for turning. That side will be sewn into the seam. The open side is indicated on the pattern piece.

HINT: For smoother curves and sharper corners, shorten the stitch on the machine. To make a nice corner, sew to the turn point, make a half-turn, and take a stitch; finish the turn and continue stitching.

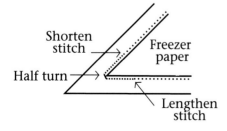

Check that the seam is smooth and looks like the shape you are making. Trim the seamline to a scant ¼", clip curves, turn, and press.

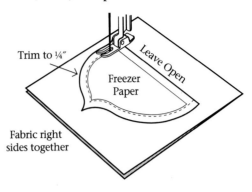

The seam into which the insert is sewn is indicated by a ★. The raw edge of the open side of the insert is matched with the raw edge of the seam.

SEWING A LOOSE INSERT INTO A FAST FORTY-FIVE

To sew an ear, prairie point, or other loose insert into a Fast Forty-Five seamline, mark the seamline on the piece to which it will be sewn (Piece #1). For a 2" Fast Forty-Five, mark 2" from the corners; for a 1½" Fast Forty-Five, mark 1½" from the corners, and so on. Connect the marks to establish the sewing line.

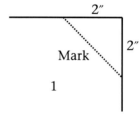

Lay the stitching line of the completed insert piece on the marked line. **The seam allowance of the insert will extend ¼" past the marked line.**

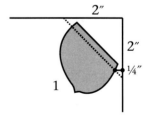

Lay the 2″ x 2″ square, that has been pressed into a triangle, over the insert and sew as you would a regular Fast Forty-Five. The insert will be sandwiched between the two fabrics.

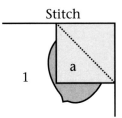

BRAIDS FOR TAILS

Inserted braids make great tails for a variety of animals. The patterns will tell you the size rectangle to cut for the braid. Divide the rectangle into three equal portions and cut as shown. Fold each section in half lengthwise, **wrong** sides together, and press. Braid, overlapping the uncut part at the top. If the edges ravel, tuck them under a bit as you braid. Finally, tie two of the ends over each other and knot. Stitch the top part of the braid into the seam. Trim the bottom ends.

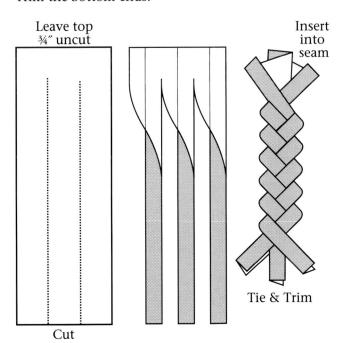

PRAIRIE POINTS

A **prairie point** is made by cutting a square then folding it on the diagonal two times. The result is a triangle with raw edges on the long side. In these patterns, prairie points are tucked into seams and make loose points for tails, sunbeams, points of fences, and so on. The width of the prairie point will be the length of one side of the original square.

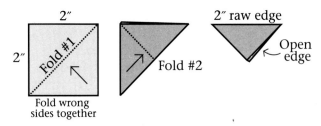

A **modified prairie point** is folded so that the two open edges meet in the front. It is used for the elephant hats. The width of the modified prairie point will be the length of one side of the original square. It is folded as shown below.

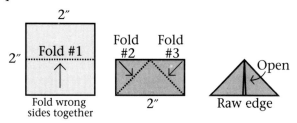

An **eight-layer prairie point** is a modified prairie point that is folded again as shown. It is used as a tail for the reindeer.

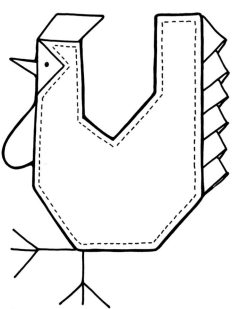

■ APPLIQUE ■

The freezer paper/spray starch method of applique is recommended for the **Tender Loving Covers**. Because many of the applique shapes on these quilts are done over pieced seams, it is not advisable to cut away under the applique. Cutting through the seams can cause them to open. The traditional needle-turn method can be done just as effectively but requires some experience. Applique patterns in this book **do not** include seam allowances.

MAKING FREEZER PAPER TEMPLATES

Freezer paper has a waxed, shiny side and a dull, paper side. When tracing each pattern onto the freezer paper, draw on the shiny side so the applique will always face in the correct direction when completed. Use a pencil or a fine permanent pen. When you trace the applique patterns marked *Cut 1, Cut 1 Reversed*, like the clown's shoe in *Under the Big Top*, trace patterns once on the **shiny** side of the freezer paper and once on the **dull** side.

Place a piece of the freezer paper over the pattern in the book and trace the shape onto the paper. Cut the shape out directly on the line. Iron the freezer paper, shiny side down, onto the **wrong side** of the fabric, making sure that there is at least ¼" of fabric showing around the paper template on all sides. Cut out the fabric following the paper shape; leave a generous ⅛" seam allowance.

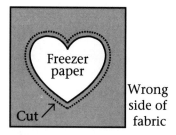

Whenever there is a curve or deep V such as the V in a heart, snip the seam allowance to the freezer paper. This allows the fabric to "give" when the seam allowance is turned under.

Spray a small amount of starch into the lid of the can. Dip the paintbrush into the starch while it is still foamy and paint the fabric **seam allowances** around the paper. Gently roll the fabric over onto the paper and press with a dry iron. It is a good idea to turn and press any points down first then fold in the sides.

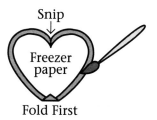

After turning under all sides, remove the freezer paper and press the applique one more time. The shaped piece is now ready to be hand stitched to the block.

The only time that an edge is not turned under is when that portion of the applique is covered by another piece of fabric (either another appliqued piece or a seam). When this occurs, leave the underneath fabric flat to prevent lumps from showing through.

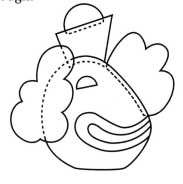

If a portion of the applique is to be sewn into a seam, line up the raw edge of the shape with the edge of the block. Do not turn under this part of the shape. When stitching this edge, use a running stitch inside the seam allowance instead of the applique stitch. The applique will be sandwiched into the seam.

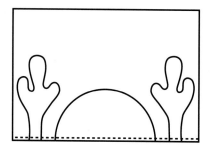

MACHINE EMBROIDERY THREAD

Because machine embroidery thread is extremely fine, it makes a nearly invisible hand applique stitch. **Caution: Machine embroidery thread is not strong enough for piecing the blocks.** Sew using a single strand of thread about 18″ long. A longer strand will tangle and break. Because the thread is so fine, gray can be used on darker shades of fabric, and natural will work well on all light pieces. Choose the thread to go with the appliqued shape, not the background.

THE APPLIQUE STITCH

The stitch used for applique is called a blind stitch or hem stitch. The goal when appliqueing is to make the stitch invisible. Tie a knot in the end of the thread. Come up from the back of the block and through the fold of the applique shape, at point A. Put the needle down directly next to A, at point B, piercing the background only. Come up at point C, a generous ⅛″ away, catching the fold of the applique again. Repeat. After stitching around the entire shape, pull the thread through to the back, take a tiny backstitch, and tie a knot. Cut the thread, leaving a ¼″ tail.

At a clipped curve, the stitches need to be close together to strengthen that area. Because the embroidery thread is so fine, it will not build up and look heavy. Make sure one stitch always comes up at a point (such as the bottom point of a heart), so that it is anchored securely.

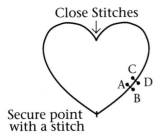

Close Stitches

Secure point with a stitch

Except for circles, the applique pieces are numbered. Applique them in numerical order. As a general rule, start with the piece that lies closest to the background fabric. Suggested fabrics and colors are given for each piece.

APPLIQUED CIRCLES

Most of the *Tender Loving Covers* have circular shapes. Freezer paper templates can be used to applique these circles, but there is an easier, more accurate alternative.

Cut circles from thin cardboard. Lay the cardboard template on the fabric and cut the fabric ¼″ larger than the circle.
1. On the **right** side, sew a running stitch around the fabric circle in the seam allowance about ⅛″ from the raw edge.
2. Lay the cardboard on the **wrong** side of the fabric.
3. Pull the ends of the threads tight and tie them together, gathering the seam allowance around the cardboard circle.

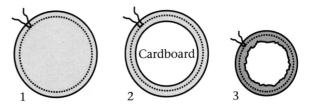

Lightly paint the edges of the circle with starch, as explained on page 12, and press the edges toward the center. Snip the thread. Remove the cardboard, and press again. Cardboard circles may be reused.

To pin a large circle in place for applique, point the sharp end of the pin toward the outside of the circle as shown.

FUSIBLE WEB AND MACHINE APPLIQUE

Fusing the applique pieces will speed the construction of the quilts and is especially useful for small designs. Trace the design onto the fusible web, fuse the web to the fabric, then cut the design on the drawn line. **Do not** add seam allowance. Follow the manufacturer's directions for fusing. Permanently attach the appliques by stitching around the fused design with a machine zigzag or buttonhole stitch.

PIECING THE BACK OF THE QUILT

Measure the completed quilt top. Plan for the backing to be 4″ larger than the quilt for easy layering.

When a quilt is wider than 45″, the backing must be pieced. The backing can be pieced either horizontally or vertically. Backings on most of the *Tender Loving Covers* are figured with seams running horizontally. It is a good idea to have two seams rather than one, giving it a more balanced, planned look, and distributing the weight of the quilt. Cut off selvages before seaming.

For a quilt 48″ x 70″, cut two lengths of 44″- 45″ wide fabric 4″ longer than the width of the quilt (52″). Cut off selvages. The quilt is 70″ long, so the backing must be 74″ long.

$$74″ - 44″ = 30″$$
$$30″ \div 2 = 15″$$
$$15″ + \tfrac{1}{2}″ \text{ for seam allowance} = 15\tfrac{1}{2}″$$

Cut one of the 52″ lengths of fabric to get two lengths that are 15½″ x 52″. Sew the 15½″ panels to the center panel as shown. On shorter quilts, it may be necessary to trim the 45″ piece so that the additional panels are not too narrow.

Top

↕ 15″

↕ 44″   74″

↕ 15″

52″

BATTING

All of the quilts in this book have been machine quilted using a needle-punched cotton batting. Cotton batting creates a flat quilt that "breathes" and feels wonderful. Needle-punched cotton batting does not need to be quilted as closely as the traditional 100% cotton batting.

Cotton batting is easy to machine quilt as it adheres well to the top and bottom layers of the quilt. The batting will shrink slightly, causing the stitches to "sink" into the quilt, thus emphasizing the quilting designs and hiding the machine stitches. Cotton batting gives quilts an "old" look and feel. If a slightly puffier look is desired, use a low-loft or regular weight polyester batting.

When fabrics and cotton batting are not prewashed, there will be significant shrinkage, up to four inches on a twin-size quilt if closely machine quilted. Allow for this shrinkage when planning bed-size quilts.

LAYERING THE QUILT

Lay the backing, centered, over a table, **wrong** side up. Stretch the backing across the table and secure it using large binder clips that can be purchased at office supply stores. Cut the batting the same size as the prepared backing. Smooth the batting over the backing, then center the quilt top on the batting **right** side up. Begin pinning in the middle of the quilt, smoothing the layers toward the outside as you go. Pin with rustproof safety pins about every 4″. Avoid pinning over the seams where you will be quilting in the ditch (seamline).

QUILTING SUGGESTIONS

Most of the quilting on the *Tender Loving Covers* was done using invisible monofilament thread. Clear thread is best for light colors, and smoke is better for dark colors because it doesn't shine. It is often necessary to **loosen** the top sewing machine tension slightly so the bobbin thread does not pull up onto the quilt top. Cotton or poly-cotton thread in a color that coordinates with the backing of the quilt works well in the bobbin. If cotton or poly-cotton thread is used on the top, match the thread to the fabric.

While machine quilting, the weight of the quilt should be supported on a table to the left and behind the sewing machine, allowing the quilt to be manipulated easily. Tightly roll the portion of the quilt to the right side of the needle so that it will fit under the machine head. "Bicycle" clips can be used to secure the rolled portion of the quilt.

Place one hand on each side of the needle and use the fingertips of both hands to manipulate the quilt. The rubber fingertip covers used to turn pages provide grip to move the quilt.

A walking foot is required for successful straight-line quilting. Always stitch on the side of the ditch away from the pressed seam allowance, slightly stretching the seam open so the stitches will not show when the fabric is released. Begin stitching in the middle of the quilt and stitch toward the outside "in the ditch". Make sure to stitch in the ditch over all loose inserts to secure them.

After quilting around each block, quilt inside the block, using the darning foot for freehand quilting. A meandered design works well to fill in large areas. Start and stop each section of quilting with ½″ of very close stitches. These short stitches will take the place of a knot.

Experiment with different designs before actually quilting. If this is a first experience with machine quilting, we suggest further reading on the subject and quilting a "practice" piece.

Metallic thread can be used for accent quilting. Use a top-stitching needle for quilting with this specialty thread so that the metal will not strip away from the thread core. The top-stitching needle has a bigger eye and groove than an all-purpose sewing machine needle.

Most of the borders on the *Tender Loving Covers* were quilted following a stencil with a continuous design. For machine quilting, following the pattern exactly is not as important as creating smooth curves and straight lines.

BINDING

After quilting, baste the three layers together inside the ¼″ seam allowance at the edge of the quilt. Trim excess batting and backing, following the straight edge of the quilt top. Use a square rotary ruler to square each corner of the quilt.

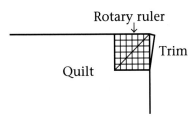

Before binding, put the quilt through a delicate cycle in warm water and spin it. Dry flat. Wetting the quilt before binding it results in a flatter edge and a smoother binding.

Successful binding is an element that gives the quilt a "finished" look. Think about the binding as a narrow frame around your work. A finished ¼″ binding is recommended.

The first thing that usually wears out on a quilt is the binding, therefore, a double binding is preferred. Cut strips 2¼″ wide on the straight grain, either lengthwise or crosswise. When it is necessary to piece the binding, it is best done on a diagonal, thus distributing the bulk of the seam allowance. To do this, overlap two 2¼″ strips **right** sides together, matching them in the corner as shown. Sew a diagonal seam. Trim, leaving a ¼″ seam allowance. Press strip lengthwise, **wrong** sides together, to 1⅛″. A binding strip should be prepared 3″ to 4″ longer than the side of the quilt to which it will be attached.

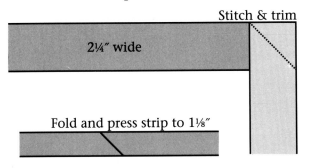

Find the middle of the quilt and the middle of the binding strip; pin the raw edges of the binding to the raw edge of the quilt, matching center points. Using a ¼″ seam allowance, stitch a strip of binding to one edge of the quilt, beginning and ending at seam intersections.

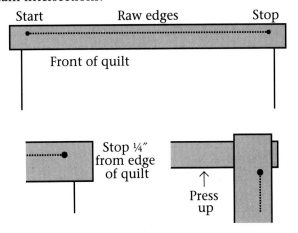

Sew strips to the other three sides; each strip shares a corner with the previously sewn strip. Press binding toward the outside of the quilt. To miter the corners, work from the right side of the quilt – fold the "top" binding strip under to form a 45° angle.

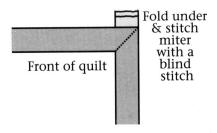

Blind-stitch the fold, beginning from the inside corner of the miter. Turn over and trim excess fabric ¼″ from blind-stitched seam. Turn the binding to the back and blind-stitch in place, folding the corners as shown.

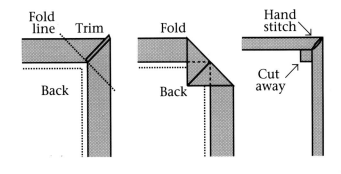

SHOOT FOR THE STARS

July 20, 1969, 10:56 p.m. EDT - Most Americans were glued to their television sets, watching our astronauts preparing for that now historic moon walk. The fantasies, dreams, and goals of earthbound man had been achieved.

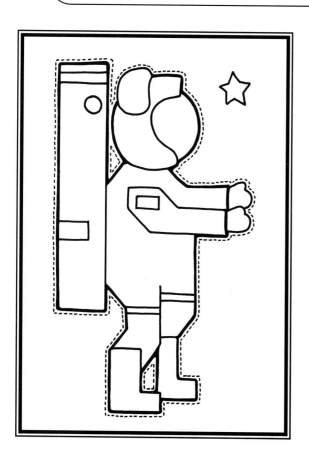

"That's one small step for a man, one giant leap for mankind." Neil Armstrong

SIZE: 40″ x 57″ (102 cm x 145 cm)

YARDAGE:
1⅓ yds. (1.3 m) blue twinkling star background
¼ yd. (.3 m) cream for space shuttle, telescope & astronaut
¼ yd. (.3 m) light blue for rockets & telescope body
¼ yd. (.3 m) light pink for ring on the Saturn planet (lamé optional)
⅛ yd. (.2 m) or scraps of light gold, medium gold & silver for astronaut's suit (lamé optional)
¼ yd. (.3 m) rose for inserted border
1¾ yds. (1.6 m) navy for border & binding
⅜ yd. (.4 m) for binding if different from border
1¾ yds. (1.6 m) backing (must be 43″ - 44″ usable width)
batting at least 44″ x 61″

Fabrics for Earth, fire, stars, fireclouds, and Saturn planet to be selected from your "stash" as discussed in *General Directions*. You will need ⅛ yd. pieces for Earth and stars. Fireclouds and Saturn require 8″ squares. Fire requires ⅛ yd. each of 4-6 plain colors.

Applique pattern pieces are on pages 112-117. Circle patterns are on page 134.

16

SHOOT FOR THE STARS
Finished Size 40″ x 57″

THE PLANET SATURN

Finished Size 32″ x 12″

CUT

Fabric/Color	Pieces	Size or #
Background/blue	#1	32½″ x 12½″
Applique Pieces (patterns on pages 112, 113, 134)		
Saturn/cardboard	6″ circle	cut 1
Saturn ring/freezer paper	#2	trace 1
Shuttle top/freezer paper	#3	trace 1
Stars/freezer paper	#4	trace 2

APPLIQUE

Position the 6″ Saturn circle and ring on the left side of the block. Refer to *General Directions, Applique*, for preparing circles. The ring should start 3″ from the left raw edge and at least ½″ from the bottom. The top part of Saturn lays over the top of the ring. The bottom of Saturn is placed under the bottom part of the ring. The shuttle top should be appliqued **after** the Saturn block is seamed to the blocks below it. Applique stars last. See *General Directions, Applique*.

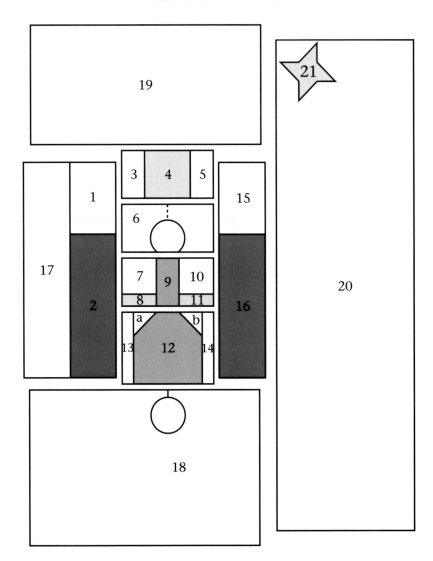

CUT

Fabric/Color	Pieces	Size or #
Background/blue	#1, 15	2½″ x 3½″
	#3, 5	1½″ x 2½″
	#6	4½″ x 2½″
	#7, 10	2″ x 2″
	#12a, 12b	1½″ x 1½″
	#13, 14	1″ x 3½″
	#17	2½″ x 9½″
	#18	10½″ x 7″
	#19	10½″ x 5½″
	#20	6½″ x 21″
Mirror, arm extensions/silver	#4	2½″ x 2½″
	#8, 11	2″ x 1″
Telescope body/lt. blue	#9	1½″ x 2½″
	#12	3½″ x 3½″
Arms/cream	#2, 16	2½″ x 6½″

Applique Pieces (patterns on pages 112, 134)

Telescope head/cardboard	1½″ circle	cut 1
Rear mirror/cardboard	1½″ circle	cut 1
Star/freezer paper	#21	trace 1

PIECE

Assemble block in units following diagram. Review construction of Fast Forty-fives in *General Directions*.

APPLIQUE

After block has been pieced, applique telescope head and rear mirror as shown. Refer to *General Directions, Applique,* for preparing circles and other techniques. Applique stars. Embroider straight lines between circles and seams as shown.

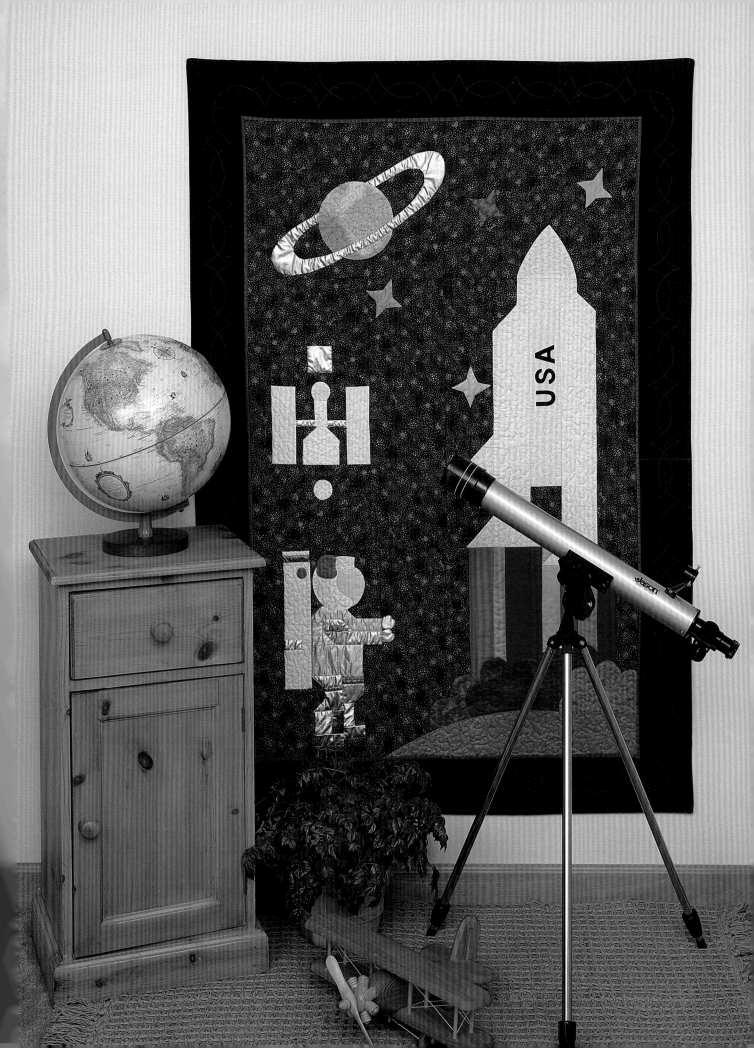

SPACE SHUTTLE

Finished Size 16″ x 20½″

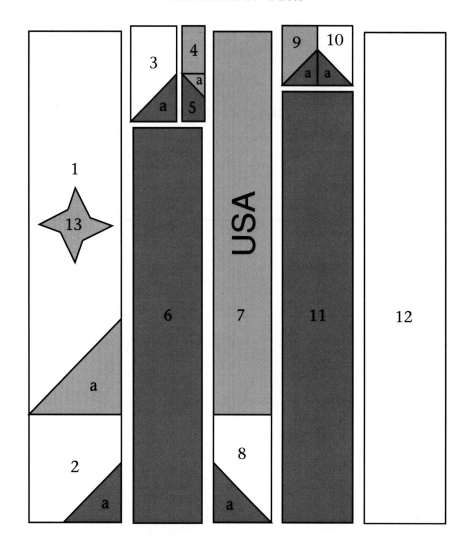

CUT

Fabric/Color	Pieces	Size or #
Background/blue	#1	4½″ x 16½″
	#2	4½″ x 5″
	#3	2½″ x 4½″
	#8	3″ x 5″
	#10	2″ x 3″
	#12	4″ x 21″
Shuttle/cream	#1a	4½″ x 4½″
	#4	1½″ x 2½″
	#5a	1½″ x 1½″
	#7	3″ x 16½″
	#9	2″ x 3″
Booster/lt. blue	#2a, 8a	3″ x 3″
	#3a	2½″ x 2½″
	#5	1½″ x 2½″
	#6	3½″ x 17″
	#9a, 10a	2″ x 2″
	#11	3½″ x 18½″

Applique Pieces (patterns on page 112)

USA lettering/fusible web		trace 1 set
Star/freezer paper	#13	trace 1

PIECE

Assemble block in units following diagram. Review construction of Fast Forty-Fives in *General Directions*.

APPLIQUE

After block has been pieced, applique star as shown. Refer to *General Directions, Applique*. Trace USA lettering in reverse on fusible web. Fuse to fabric, then cut out letters on drawn lines. Stitch around letters with zigzag or buttonhole stitch.

THE ASTRONAUT
Finished Size 10″ x 16½″

CUT

Fabric/Color	Pieces	Size or #
Background/blue	#7	2¾″ x 6½″
	#8	6¼″ x 4¾″
	#9a, 26a	1¼″ x 1¼″
	#9b	1½″ x 1½″
	#10	2½″ x 1½″
	#17	1½″ x 3¼″
	#21	1½″ x 2¼″
	#28	1¼″ x 2¼″
	#30	2¼″ x 1″
	#32	2″ x 8¼″
	#33	6¼″ x 2″
	#34	2½″ x 17″
Astronaut/lt. gold	#11	1½″ x 1″
	#13	1″ x 1½″
	#14a, 17a, 17b, 21a	1½″ x 1½″
	#15	5¼″ x 1½″
	#18	2″ x 1½″
	#20	2″ x 2″
Astronaut/med. gold	#9	4¼″ x 1½″
	#14	3¾″ x 1½″
	#15a	1½″ x 1½″
	#16	1½″ x 2½″
	#24	2¼″ x 1″
	#26	2¼″ x 2″
	#31	4¾″ x 2¾″
Backpack/cream	#1	2¾″ x 1″
	#3	2¾″ x 6¼″
	#5	1¼″ x 1¼″
	#6	2¾″ x 3½″
Boots, backpack/silver	#4	2″ x 1¼″
	#22	2″ x 2¼″
	#23	3″ x 1½″
	#27	1½″ x 2¼″
	#29	2¼″ x 1½″
Stripes/pink	#2	2¾″ x 1″
	#12	1½″ x 1″
	#19	2″ x ¾″
	#25	2¼″ x ¾″

Applique Pieces (patterns on pages 113, 134)

Face shield/freezer paper	#35	trace 1
Helmet/freezer paper	#36	trace 1
Transmitter/freezer paper	#37	trace 1
Backpack circle/cardboard	¾″ circle	cut 1
Hands/freezer paper	#38	trace 2

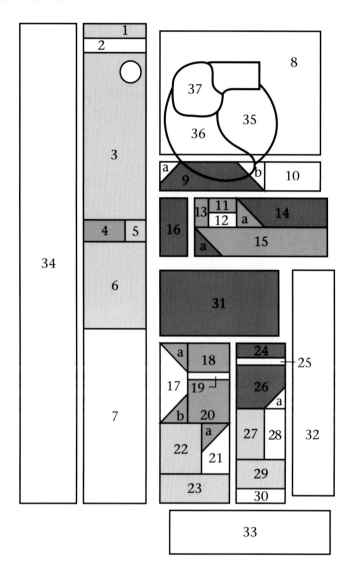

PIECE

Assemble block in units following diagram. Review construction of Fast Forty-Fives in *General Directions* (1a, 1b, ect.).

APPLIQUE

After block has been pieced, applique astronaut's helmet and backpack circle as shown in diagram. Refer to *General Directions, Applique,* for preparing circles and other techniques. Applique hands after the astronaut is sewn to the Ignition Liftoff block.

Continued on page 80.

E-I-E-I-O

The ingredients of a great culture are inherent in the family farm: a sense of community and interdependence, the tendency to work and play hard, the passing on to future generations of values such as strength of character, honesty, and faith in God.

Watch your thoughts, they become words. Watch your words, they become actions. Watch your habits, they become character. Watch your character, it becomes your destiny. Frank Outlaw

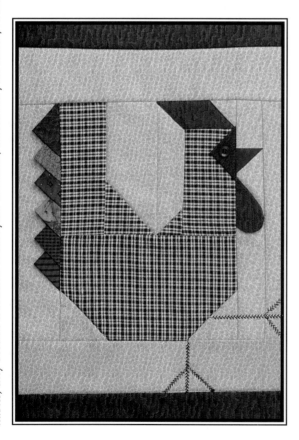

SIZE: 53"x 68" (135 cm x 173 cm)
For twin size adjustments, see page 26.

YARDAGE:
⅛ yd. (.2 m) blue background for sheep
12" square (31 x 31 cm) lt. gold background for sun
½ yd. (.5 m) cream print background for corn, tractor, wagon, barn, & hen
⅓ yd. (.3 m) cream solid background for rooster & cow
⅛ yd. (.2 m) tan stripe background for pigs
¼ yd. (.3 m) pink for pigs
⅓ yd. (.3 m) plaid for cow
¼ yd. (.3 m) dark brown for wheels & trims
⅝ yd. (.6 m) medium brown for picket fence
⅛ yd. pregathered ribbon for pig's tail
2 yds. (1.9 m) green for border & sashing
⅝ yd. (.6 m) red for binding
3¼ yds. (3 m) backing (pieced horizontally)
batting at least 57" x 72"

From your stash, choose 9" squares of plaid for the wagon and the sun. For remaining fabrics, you will need ⅛ yd. pieces or less. See *General Directions*.

Applique, loose insert, and patchwork pattern pieces are on pages 118, 119. Circle patterns are on page 134.

25

E-I-E-I-O
Finished Size 53″ x 68″

TWIN SIZE: 67″ x 82″
Yardage:
  2½ yds. (2.3 m) for additional border
  ¾ yd. (.7 m) for binding
  5 yds. (4.6 m) for backing (pieced vertically)
Cut two borders 7½″ x 82½″ and sew to sides of quilt.
Cut two borders 7½″ x 67½″ and sew to top and bottom of quilt.
Miter corners. We recommend that this border be made of the
same fabric as the background of the fence border.

26

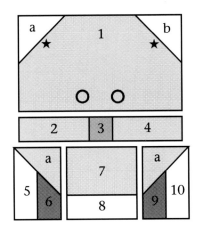

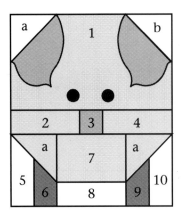

Cutting chart is for one block only. **Make two blocks.**

CUT

Fabric/Color	Pieces	Size or #
Bkgrnd./tan stripe	#1a, 1b	2½″ x 2½″
	#5, 10	1½″ x 3½″
	#8	3½″ x 1½″
Body/pink	#1	7½″ x 4½″
	#2, 4	3½″ x 1½″
	#5/6a, 9/10a	2½″ x 2½″
	#7	3½″ x 2½″
Legs/brown	#6, 9	1½″ x 3½″
Nose/dark pink	#3	1½″ x 1½″
Applique Piece (pattern on page 134)		
Eyes/cardboard	⅝″ circle	cut 1
Loose Insert (pattern on page 118)		
Ears/freezer paper	ear	trace 2

PIECE

Review Fast Forty-Fives and sewing loose inserts into Fast Forty-Fives in *General Directions*. Make two ears, referring to loose inserts section of *General Directions*. Assemble block in units following diagram. Stitch ears, facing in, into the seams indicated by stars in the diagram. Sew #5 and #6 together and then do a Fast Forty-Five as shown. Repeat for 9/10 except sew Fast Forty-Five on opposite corner.

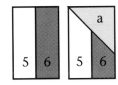

APPLIQUE

Applique two eyes or stitch on buttons. Refer to *General Directions, Applique*, for preparing circles.

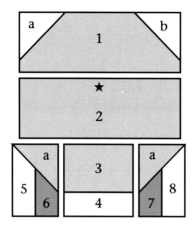

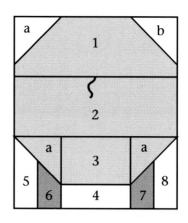

CUT

Fabric/Color	Pieces	Size or #
Bkgrnd./tan stripe	#1a, 1b	2½″ x 2½″
	#4	3½″ x 1½″
	#5, 8	1½″ x 3½″
Body/pink	#1, 2	7½″ x 3″
	#3	3½″ x 2½″
	#5/6a, 7/8a	2½″ x 2½″
Legs/brown	#6, 7	1½″ x 3½″
Loose Insert		
Tail/pregathered ribbon	3″	cut 1

PIECE

Review construction of Fast Forty-Fives in *General Directions* (1a, 1b, etc.). Assemble block in units following diagram. When piecing 5/6, sew 5 and 6 together and then do a Fast Forty-Five as shown. See diagrams in Hello Piggy piecing instructions. Repeat for 7/8 except sew Fast Forty-Five on opposite corner. Stitch ribbon into seam indicated by star in diagram.

ASSEMBLE ROW

Stitch Goodbye Piggy between the two Hello Piggy blocks. Row should measure 8½″ x 21½″.

Cutting chart is for one block only. **Make two blocks, one in reverse.**

CUT

Fabric/Color	Pieces	Size or #
Bkgrnd./dark blue	#2, 3	3½″ x 1″
	#4, 5	1″ x 4½″
Body/blue & tan plaid	#1	3½″ x 3½″
Loose Insert		
Beak/prairie point	1½″ x 1½″	cut 1

PIECE

Make prairie point for beak, referring to prairie points directions in loose inserts section of *General Directions*. Assemble block following diagram. Stitch beak into seam indicated by star on diagram. **Hint:** To make the reversed block, stitch the beak between #1 and #5 instead of #1 and #4. Machine or hand embroider feet. Embroider or sew on a small button for eye.

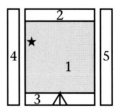

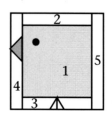

This House Is Full Of Love

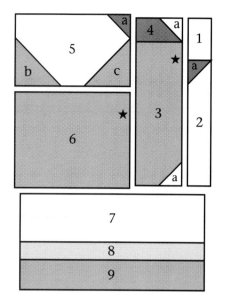

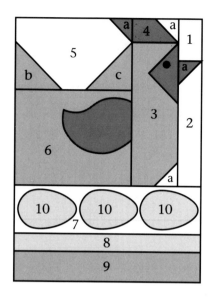

CUT

Fabric/Color	Pieces	Size or #
Bkgrnd./cream print	#1	1½" x 2¼"
	#2	1½" x 5¾"
	#3a, 4a	1½" x 1½"
	#5	5½" x 3½"
	#7	8½" x 2½"
Body/gray	#3	2½" x 6½"
	#5b, 5c	2½" x 2½"
	#6	5½" x 4½"
Comb & beak/red	#2a, 5a	1½" x 1½"
	#4	2½" x 1½"
Hay/red & tan stripe	#8	8½" x 1¼"
Nest/straw color	#9	8½" x 1¾"
Applique Piece (pattern on page 118)		
Eggs/freezer paper	#10	trace 3
Loose Inserts (pattern on page 118)		
Wing/freezer paper	wing	trace 1
Face/prairie point	2½" x 2½"	cut 1

PIECE

Make wing, referring to loose inserts section of *General Directions*. Make prairie point for face, referring to prairie points directions in loose inserts section of *General Directions*. Assemble block in units following diagram, stitching face and wing into seams indicated by stars in diagram. Review construction of Fast Forty-Fives in *General Directions* (1a, 1b, etc.). Embroider an eye or sew on a small button through "face" (loose insert prairie point).

APPLIQUE

Applique eggs to #7, referring to *General Directions, Applique*.

CUT

Fabric/Color	Pieces	Size or #
Bkgrnd./lt. brown	#1, 3, 4, 6, 7, 9	1½″ x 1½″
	#2, 8	2½″ x 1½″
Foreground/green	#1a, 3a, 7a, 9a	1½″ x1½″
	#5	2½″ x 1½″

PIECE

Assemble block in units following diagram. Review construction of Fast Forty-Fives in *General Directions* (1a, 1b, etc.). Stitch a chick to the top and bottom of this block, creating a vertical unit measuring 4½″ x 11½″.

CUT

Fabric/Color	Pieces	Size or #
Bkgrnd./light gold	#1	10½″ x 10½″
Applique Piece (pattern on page 134)		
Sun/cardboard	6″ circle	cut 1
Loose Insert		
Sun rays/prairie points	2½″ x 2½″	cut 12

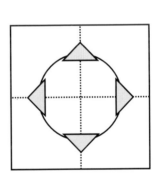

APPLIQUE

Make sun's rays, referring to prairie points directions in loose inserts section of *General Directions*. Press block into quarters. Draw a 6″ circle centered on the background block. Pin one prairie point on each fold line so that the seam allowance extends ¼″ into the circle. Evenly space two prairie points between each two of the pinned prairie points, tucking them inside each other. Machine baste the prairie points just inside the drawn circle. Applique the 6″ circle over the prairie points, referring to *General Directions, Applique*.

Continued on page 83.

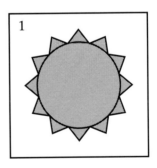

WHEELS & MORE WHEELS

Wherever one finds a little boy, one is sure to find little cars bulging from pockets, peeking from under chairs, caught between cushions, always underfoot. Yet they never have too many.

Little boys, little toys. Big boys, big toys.

SIZE: 54½"x 63" (139 cm x 160 cm)
For twin size adjustments, see page 34.

YARDAGE:
½ yd. (.5 m) light check for bkgrnd. of dump truck
⅓ yd. (.3 m) each of 4 light checks for backgrounds
   of other cars & trucks
⅓ yd. (.3 m) black for wheels, hook, signs
⅛ yd. (.2 m) red for emergency lights
⅛ yd. (.2 m) cream for windows
1 yd. (1 m) ¼" black grosgrain ribbon for tow truck
1⅝ yds. (1.5 m) teal check for border
⅝ yd. (.6 m) for binding
3½ yds. (3.2 m) backing (pieced horizontally)
batting at least 58" x 67"

Remainder of fabrics for cars and trucks to be selected from your stash as discussed in *General Directions*. You will need ⅛ yd. pieces or less.

Applique pattern pieces are on page 120. Circle patterns are on page 134.

FABRIC-CHOOSING HINTS
Gather your stash. Separate coordinating blues, reds, greens, tans, and teals. For each fire truck and dump truck, you will need three coordinating fabrics. For each ambulance, police car, and tow truck, you will need two fabrics. In this quilt, each vehicle was made with a different combination of fabrics, however, it could be just as pleasing to repeat the same fabric combinations throughout the row.

POLICE CAR
Finished Size 9″ x 4½″

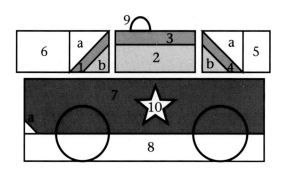

Cutting chart is for sashing strips and one block only. **Make four blocks.**

CUT (*cut first)

Fabric/Color	Piece or #	Size or #
Bkgrnd./lt. green ck. (sashing)	*cut 1	43″ x 5″
	cut 2	1½″ x 5″
	cut 3	2″ x 5″
Bkgrnd./lt. green ck. (block)	#1a, 4a	2″ x 2″
	#5	1½″ x 2″
	#6	2½″ x 2″
	#7a	1″ x 1″
	#8	9½″ x 1½″
Car top/green plaid	#1, 4	2″ x 2″
	#3	3½″ x 1″
Car body/med. green	#7	9½″ x 2½″
Windows/cream	#1b, 4b	1½″ x 1½″
	#2	3½″ x 1½″
Applique Pieces (patterns on pages 120, 134)		
Wheels/cardboard	2″ circle	cut 1
Emer. light/freezer paper	#9	trace 1
Star/fusible web	#10	trace 1

PIECE
Assemble four blocks in units following diagram. Review construction of Fast Forty-Fives in *General Directions* (1a, 1b, etc.).

ASSEMBLE ROW
Sew row as shown. Sew the 43″ x 5″ strip to top of row.

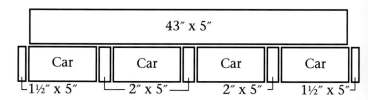

APPLIQUE
Refer to *General Directions, Applique*, for preparing circles. Applique wheels ¼″ from the raw edge at the bottom of the block to allow for the seam allowance. Applique emergency light. Using fusible applique technique in *General Directions*, attach a star to each police car. Zigzag to secure. Optional: Sew gold beads on points of stars.

AMBULANCE

Finished Size 12½″ x 6″

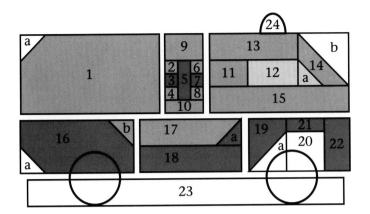

Cutting chart is for sashing and one block only.
Make three blocks.

CUT (*cut first)

Fabric/Color	Piece or #	Size or #
Bkgrnd./tan check (sashing)	*cut 1	43″ x 4½″
	cut 2	1½″ x 6½″
	cut 2	2″ x 6½″
Bkgrnd./tan check (block)	#1a, 16a	1½″ x 1½″
	#14b	2½″ x 2½″
	#19a, 20	2″ x 2″
	#23	13″ x 1½″
Upper van/brown or gold	#1	6″ x 3½″
	#2, 4, 6, 8	1″ x 1″
	#9, 11	2″ x 1½″
	#10	2″ x 1″
	#13	4″ x 1½″
	#14	2½″ x 2½″
	#15	6″ x 1½″
	#16b	1½″ x 1½″
	#17	4½″ x 1½″
Lower van/brown plaid	#16	5″ x 2½″
	#17a	1½″ x 1½″
	#18	4½″ x 1½″
	#19	2″ x 2½″
	#21	2″ x 1″
	#22	1½″ x 2½″
Windows/cream	#12	2½″ x 1½″
	#14a	1½″ x 1½″
Medical cross/brn. or gold	#3, 7	1″ x 1″
	#5	1″ x 2″

Applique Pieces (patterns on pages 120, 134)

Wheels/cardboard	2″ circle	cut 1
Emer. light/freezer paper	#24	trace 1

PIECE

Assemble three blocks in units following diagram. Review construction of Fast Forty-Fives in *General Directions* (1a, 1b, etc.).

ASSEMBLE ROW

Sew row as shown. Sew 43″ x 4½″ strip to top of row.

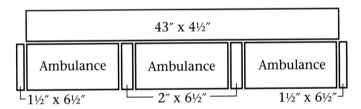

APPLIQUE

Applique wheels ¼″ from the raw edge at the bottom of the block to allow for the seam allowance. Refer to *General Directions*, *Applique*, for preparing circles and other techniques. Applique emergency light.

Continued on page 90.

A COWBOY NEEDS A QUILT

Stetson hats, boots, gritty warm winds, a rodeo queen, clowns in a barrel...ingredients of the West's hometown rodeo. In the arena, the cowboy finishes his ride or gets thrown, loops the calf or loses it, flips the steer or misses it. He picks up his hat, dusts himself off, and ambles toward the gates, thinking about another weekend, another town, and another rodeo.

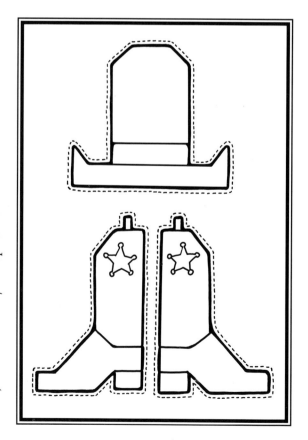

I am a great believer in luck, and I find the harder I work, the more I have of it. Stephen Leacock

SIZE: 52″ x 64″ (132 cm x 163 cm)
For twin size adjustments, see page 42.

YARDAGE:
1 yd. (1 m) blue for sky background
1 yd. (1 m) tan for background
⅓ yd. (.3 m) dark teal check for mountains
¼ yd. (.3 m) dark brown for bronco's mane
¼ yd. (.3 m) dark plaid for steer's face
⅓ yd. (.3 m) brown plaid for bronco
10″ square or ¼ yd. (.3 m) dark rose for sunset
¼ yd. (.3 m) brown for ten gallon hats
¼ yd. fringe 1″ wide for eyelashes
⅜ yd. ¼″ grosgrain ribbon or scrap of ultrasuede
1⅝ yds. (1.5 m) teal for border & binding
   ½ yd. (.5 m) for binding if different from border
3⅛ yds. (2.8 m) backing (pieced horizontally)
batting at least 56″ x 68″

Remainder of fabrics to be selected from your stash as discussed in *General Directions*. You will need ⅛ yd. pieces or less.

Applique and loose insert pattern pieces are on pages 121, 122.

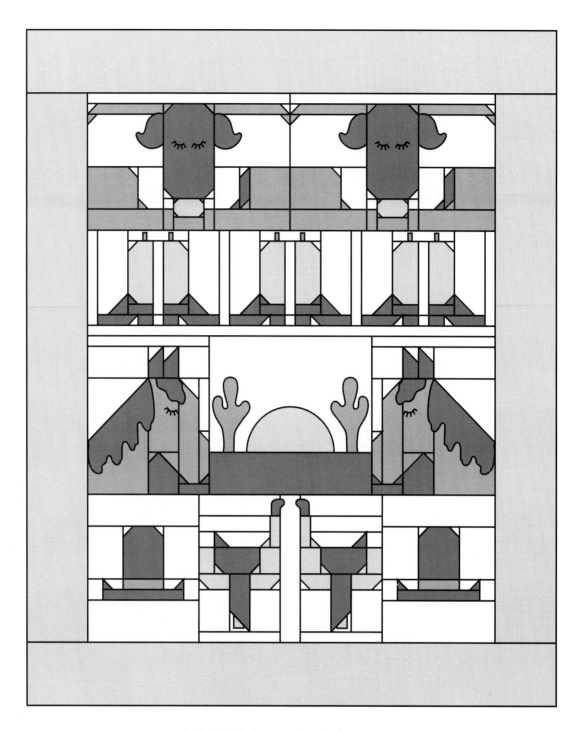

A COWBOY NEEDS A QUILT
Finished Size 52″ x 64″

TWIN SIZE: 68″ x 88″ (no pillow tuck)
Yardage:
   2¼ yds. (2.1 m) for additional border
   ¾ yd. (.7 m) for binding
   5¼ yds. (4.8 m) for backing (pieced vertically)
Cut two borders 8½″ x 68½″ and sew to sides of quilt.
Cut two borders 12½″ x 68½″ and sew to top and bottom of quilt.

Longhorn Steer
Finished Size 20″ x 13″

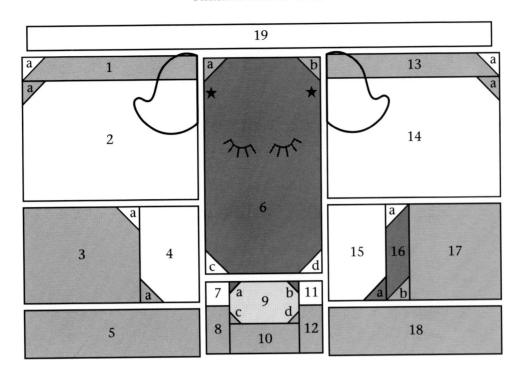

Cutting chart is for one block only. **Make two blocks.**

CUT

Fabric/Color	Pieces	Size or #
Bkgrnd./blue sky	#1a, 3a, 6c, 6d,	
	7, 11, 13a, 16a	1½″ x 1½″
	#2, 14	8″ x 5½″
	#4, 15	3″ x 4½″
	#19	20½″ x 1½″
Mtn. shadow/navy	#15a	1½″ x 1½″
	#16	1½″ x 4½″
Mountain/dk. teal ck.	#3	5½″ x 4½″
	#4a, 16b	1½″ x 1½″
	#5, 18	8″ x 2½″
	#8, 12	1½″ x 2½″
	#9c, 9d	1″ x 1″
	#10	3½″ x 1¾″
	#17	4½″ x 4½″
Steer face/dark plaid	#6	5½″ x 9½″
	#9a, 9b	1″ x 1″
Steer nose/tan	#9	3½″ x 2¼″
Horns/brown	#1, 13	8″ x 1½″
	#2a, 6a, 6b, 14a	1½″ x 1½″
Eyelashes/1″ fringe	1″	cut 2
Loose Insert (pattern on page 121)		
Ear/freezer paper	ear	trace 2

PIECE

Review construction of Fast Forty-Fives in *General Directions* (1a, 1b, etc.). Make ears, referring to loose inserts section of *General Directions*. Assemble two blocks in units following diagram, stitching ears into seams as indicated by stars on diagram. Topstitch two 1″ fringe pieces onto the face for eyes. Sew the blocks together, forming a row measuring 40½″ x 13½″.

COWBOY BOOTS

Finished Size 12″ x 9″

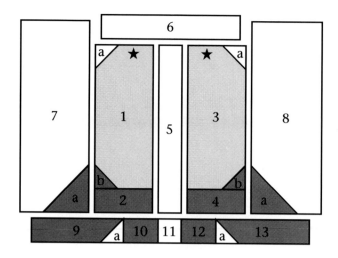

Cutting chart is for one block only. **Make three blocks.**

CUT (*cut first)

Fabric/Color	Piece or #	Size or #
Bkgrnd./tan (sashing)	*cut 1	40½″ x 1½″
	cut 4	1½″ x 9½″
Bkgrnd./tan	#1a, 3a, 9a,	
	11, 13a	1½″ x 1½″
	#5	1½″ x 7½″
	#6	6½″ x 1½″
	#7, 8	3½″ x 8½″
Boot top/plaid	#1, 3	3″ x 6½″
Boot bottom/burgundy	#1b, 3b	1½″ x 1½″
	#2, 4	3″ x 1½″
	#7a, 8a	2½″ x 2½″
	#9, 13	4½″ x 1½″
Heel/dark brown	#10, 12	2″ x 1½″
Loose Insert		
Boot loop/¼″ ribbon or ultrasuede	2″	cut 2

PIECE

Review construction of Fast Forty-Fives in *General Directions* (1a, 1b, etc.). Assemble three blocks in units following diagram. Stitch boot loops of ribbon or ultrasuede into seam indicated by stars on diagram. Press seam toward boot.

ASSEMBLE ROW

Assemble row as shown. Sew 40½″ x 1½″ strip to bottom of row. Row should measure 40½″ x 10½″.

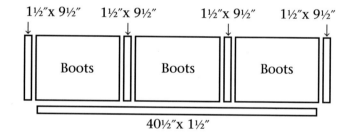

BUCKING BRONCO

Finished Size 12″ x 15″

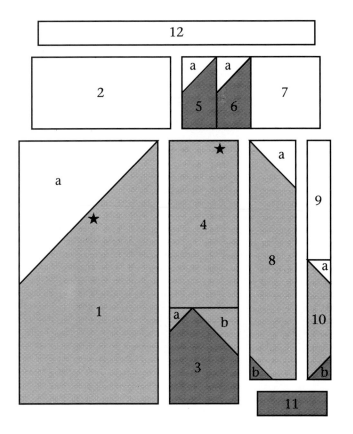

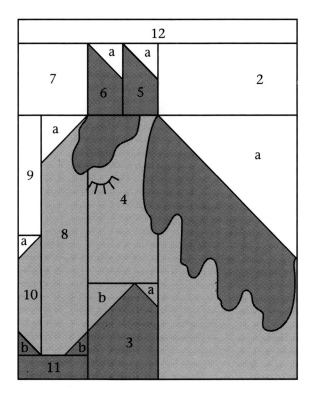

Cutting chart is for one block only. **Make one block and one block reversed.**

CUT

Fabric/Color	Pieces	Size or #
Bkgrnd./blue sky	#1a	6½″ x 6½″
	#2	6½″ x 3½″
	#5a, 6a	2″ x 2″
	#7	3½″ x 3½″
	#8a	2½″ x 2½″
	#9	1½″ x 5½″
	#10a	1½″ x 1½″
	#12	12½″ x 1½″
Bronco/med. plaid	#1	6½″ x 11½″
	#3a	1½″ x 1½″
	#3b	2½″ x 2½″
	#4	3½″ x 7½″
	#8	2½″ x 10½″
	#10	1½″ x 5½″
Field/green	#3	3½″ x 4½″
	#8b, 10b	1½″ x 1½″
	#11	3½″ x 1½″
Horse ears/dark plaid	#5, 6	2″ x 3½″

Eyelashes/1″ fringe	1″	cut 1
Loose Inserts (patterns on page 121)		
Mane/freezer paper	mane	trace 1
Forelock/freezer paper	forelock	trace 1

PIECE

Review construction of Fast Forty-Fives and stitching loose inserts into Fast-Forty-Fives in *General Directions* (1a, 1b, etc.). Make mane and forelock, referring to loose inserts section of *General Directions*. Assemble block in units following diagram, stitching mane and forelock into seams indicated by stars in diagram. Make second block in reverse.

APPLIQUE

Stitch on a 1″ piece of fringe for eye.

WESTERN SUNSET
Finished Size 16″ x 15″

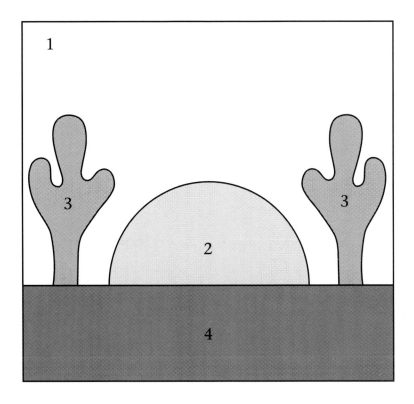

CUT

Fabric/Color	Pieces	Size or #
Bkgrnd./blue sky	#1	16½″ x 11½″
Field/green	#4	16½″ x 4½″
Applique Pieces (patterns on page 122)		
Sun/freezer paper	#2	trace 1
Cactus/freezer paper	#3	trace 1, trace 1 reversed

APPLIQUE
Applique sun and cacti to #1. Do not turn under bottom seam allowances; they should be even with the bottom seam allowance of #1. See *General Directions, Applique.*

PIECE
Stitch #4 to bottom of sun/cacti unit.

ASSEMBLE ROW
Assemble the row of broncos and sunset as shown. Row should measure 40½″ x 15½″.

Continued on page 93.

UNDER THE BIG TOP

Which is more exciting, going to the circus and watching the performers or going down to the train and watching the animals unload? The elephants all take hold of each others' tails and lead the way!

A smile on the outside puts a smile on the inside.

SIZE: 62″ x 86″ (158 cm x 219 cm)
Twin without pillow tuck

YARDAGE:
1¾ yds. (1.6 m) tan for background
1¾ yds. (1.6 m) red for tent top and sides
⅝ yd. (.6 m) blue for background of stars
Two 8″ (20 cm) squares brown for lions' faces
Two 6″ (16 cm) squares cream for clowns' faces
2¾ yds. (2.6 m) dark blue for outer borders
  & sky triangles
⅔ yd. (.6 m) dark red for binding
3¾ yds. (3.5 m) backing (pieced horizontally)
5 colors ¼″ grosgrain ribbon, ¼ yd. (.3 m) each
batting at least 66″ x 90″

From your "stash", choose fabrics for balloons, balls, elephants, ears, stands, tails, clowns, lions, cage, and stars. See *General Directions*. You will need ⅛ yd. pieces or less.

Applique and loose insert pattern pieces are on pages 123, 124. Circle patterns are on page 134.

UNDER THE BIG TOP
Finished Size 62″ x 86″
This quilt does not have pillow tuck.

BACKGROUND FABRIC (TAN)

Before using this fabric to piece the blocks, cut the following:

Two 1½" x 57½" strips from the length of the fabric. These background strips go on either side of the assembled rows of blocks to complete the inner portion of the quilt.

Six 1½" x 30½" strips to be used later for assembling the rows of stars.

One 10½" x 17½" block to be used for the background of the balloon block.

The remaining fabric is to be used for piecing the blocks.

TENT FABRIC (RED)

Tent Sides

Cut 2 strips 4½" x 57½" from the length of the fabric.

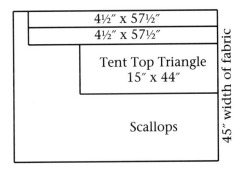

Tent Top Triangle

Cut a rectangle 15" x 44" as shown above. With **right** sides together, fold fabric in half (15" x 22"). Square up edges and press. Mark a seamline ¼" from the bottom edge of the rectangle. Measure up 12" from this seamline (A) and make a mark (B) on the fold. Measure along bottom seamline 20" from fold and make a mark (C). Draw a line connecting B and C. Mark a cutting line ¼" outside this seamline, extending it to the edge of the fabric. Cut along this line. Open up the triangle. You should now have a 120° triangle.

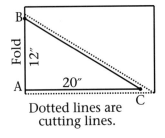

Dotted lines are
cutting lines.

SKY TRIANGLES AND BORDERS (BLUE)

Borders

Cut the following border strips from the length of the fabric:

Two strips 11½" x 69½"
One strip 11½" x 62½"
One strip 6½" x 62½"

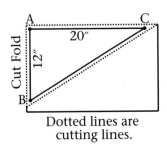

Sky Triangle

Cut a rectangle 15" x 45" as shown above. Fold **right** sides together, square up edges, and press. Mark a seamline ¼" from top edge of fabric. Mark a seamline ¼" in from the fold at the left side. Mark point A at intersection of the two seamlines. Measure 12" down from point A and mark point B. Mark point C 20" from point A along top seamline. Draw a line connecting point B to point C (seamline). Mark cutting line ¼" outside B/C and extend it to the top edge of the fabric. Cut along this line. Open up the fabric and cut directly on the pressed fold. You should now have two triangles for the sky.

Dotted lines are
cutting lines.

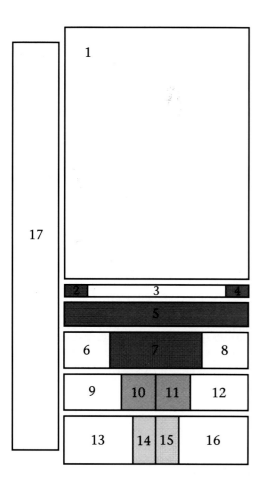

Cutting chart is for one block only. **Make one block and one block in reverse.**

CUT

Fabric/Color	Pieces	Size or #
Background/tan	#1	8½″ x 11″
	#3	6½″ x 1″
	#6, 8	2½″ x 2″
	#9, 12	3″ x 2″
	#13, 16	3½″ x 2½″
	#17	2½″ x 17½″
Shirt/red dot	#2, 4	1½″ x 1″
	#5	8½″ x 1½″
	#7	4½″ x 2″
Pants/plaid	#10, 11	2″ x 2″
Socks/blue	#14, 15	1½″ x 2½″

Applique Pieces (patterns on pages 123, 134)

Hat top/freezer paper	#18	trace 1
Hat/freezer paper	#19	trace 1
Hair/freezer paper	#20, 22	trace 1
Face/freezer paper	#21	trace 1
Outside lips/freezer paper	#23	trace 1
Inside lips/freezer paper	#24	trace 1
Eyes/cardboard	⅝″ circle	cut 1
Eyebrow/freezer paper	#25	trace 1
Nose/cardboard	2″ circle	cut 1
Suspender/freezer paper	#26	trace 2
Shoes/freezer paper	#27	trace 1, trace 1 reversed
Juggling balls/cardboard	1⅜″ circle	cut 1

PIECE

Assemble one block in units following diagram. Make a second block in reverse by attaching piece 17 to the right side of the block.

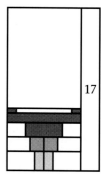

Juggling Clown applique instructions are on page 54.

APPLIQUE

Draw one set of clown face pieces on the shiny side of the freezer paper, then draw a second set of pieces on the dull side of the freezer paper. Make one clown face to your left (on block with #17 on right) and one clown face to your right (on block with #17 on left). Center face on bottom seam of piece #3. Applique suspenders. Applique one shoe and reverse one. Applique juggling balls to clown blocks after the row of clowns and balloons has been sewn together. Refer to *General Directions*, *Applique*, for preparing circles.

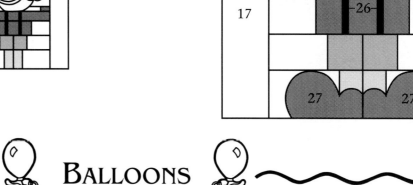

BALLOONS
Finished Size 10″ x 17″

CUT

Fabric/Color	Pieces	Size or #
Background/tan	#1	10½″ x 17½″
Applique Pieces (patterns on page 124)		
Balloon/freezer paper	#2	trace 5
Balloon tail/freezer paper	#3	trace 5
Strings/¼″ ribbon	9″	cut 5

APPLIQUE

Fold balloon block lengthwise to find center. Layer the balloons as shown. Position outside balloons 1¼″ from sides of block. Position center balloon on center fold with bottom of balloon about 8½″ from bottom of block. Applique balloon tail first, leaving the bottom edge unattached for inserting ribbon. Tuck end of ¼″ grosgrain ribbon under unattached edge of each tail. Overlap ribbons at the center fold at the bottom of the block. Stitch along both sides of each ribbon, then across the unattached balloon tail. Applique balloons.

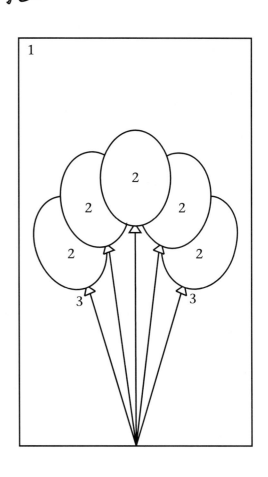

FEARSOME AND FEROCIOUS

Finished Size 9″ x 10″

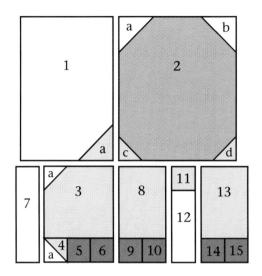

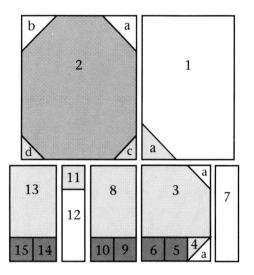

Cutting chart is for one block only. **Make two blocks, one in reverse as shown.**

CUT

Fabric/Color	Pieces	Size or #
Background/tan	#1	4½″ x 6½″
	#2a, 2b	2″ x 2″
	#3a, 4a	1½″ x 1½″
	#7	1½″ x 4½″
	#12	1½″ x 3½″
Mane/dark brown	#2	5½″ x 6½″
Body/brown ck.	#1a	2″ x 2″
	#2c, 2d, 11	1½″ x 1½″
	#8, 13	2½″ x 3½″
Back legs/gold	#3	3½″ x 3½″
	#4	1½″ x 1½″
Paws/blacks	#5, 6, 9, 10, 14, 15	1½″ x 1½″
Applique Pieces (patterns on pages 124, 134)		
Face/freezer paper	#16	trace 1
Tongue/freezer paper	#17	trace 1
Cheeks/freezer paper	#18	trace 2
Eyes/cardboard	½″ circle	cut 1
Loose Insert (pattern on page 124)		
Ears/freezer paper	ear	trace 2

PIECE

Assemble one block in units following diagram. Make another block in reverse. Review construction of Fast Forty-Fives (1a, 1b, etc.) in *General Directions.*

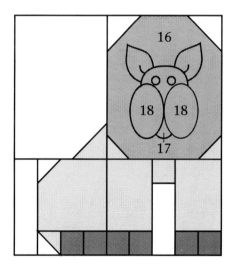

APPLIQUE

Make ears, referring to loose inserts section of *General Directions.* Applique face and tongue, tucking in the two loose, pleated ears. Applique the cheeks and finally the eyes (buttons may be substituted). Refer to *General Directions, Applique,* for preparing circles.

Continued on page 96.

READING, 'RITING, & RECESS

A large city school, a small town elementary school, or a one-room country school, all evoke a thread of common memories: the discovery that learning is both exciting and tedious, recess both fun and painful, friendships both brief and life-long. School, not only a child's first "job", but perhaps the most important one of a lifetime.

We must view young people not as bottles to be filled, but as candles to be lit. Robert H. Schaffer

SIZE: 56″ x 64″ (143 cm x 163 cm)

YARDAGE:

⅝ yd. (.6 m) cream print background #1
⅞ yd. (.8 m) cream print background #2
⅝ yd. (.6 m) cream print background #3
¼ yd. (.3 m) hot pink for apples & stop sign
¼ yd. (.3 m) turquoise for desk & playground
⅓ yd. (.3 m) black print for blackboard
⅓ yd. (.3 m) medium green for school
1¾ yds. (1.6 m) black print for border & binding
  ½ yd. (.5 m) for binding if different from border
3¾ yds. (3.7 m) backing (pieced horizontally)
¼ yd. (.3 m) brown grosgrain ribbon ¼″ wide
batting at least 60″ x 68″

From your "stash", choose fabrics at least 9″ square for hair, dress, shirt, sun, and background for George Washington. See *General Directions*. You will need ⅛ yd. or less of the remaining fabrics.

Applique and loose insert pattern pieces are on pages 125-130. Circle patterns are on page 134.

READING, 'RITING, & RECESS
Finished Size 56" x 64"

CITY SCHOOL
Finished Size 25″ x 19″

*Note: Stitch #21 to the top of the block

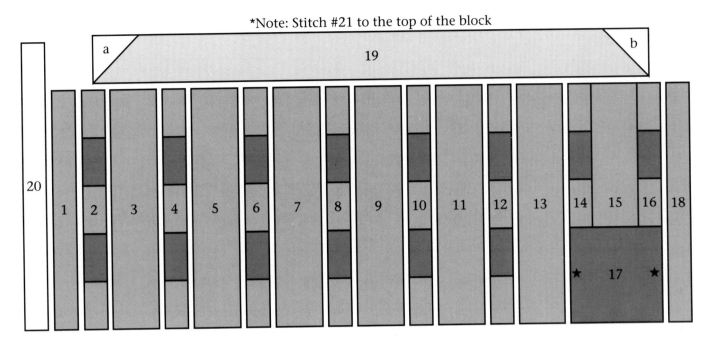

CUT

Fabric/Color	Pieces	Size or #
Background/ cream print #1	#19a, 19b	2½″ x 2½″
	#20	1½″ x 12½″
	#21*	25½″ x 7½″
Building/med. green	#1, 18	1½″ x 10½″
	#3, 5, 7, 9, 11, 13	2½″ x 10½″
	#15	2½″ x 6½″
Doorway/dk. green	#17	4½″ x 4½″
Roof/gold	#19	24½″ x 2½″
Window unit (2, 4, 6, 8, 10, 12, 14, 16)		
med. green	2½″ x 14″	cut 3
dk. green	2½″ x 14″	cut 2
Applique Pieces (patterns on page 125)		
Clouds/freezer paper	#22, 23	trace 1 each
Loose Insert		
Doors	4½″ x 4½″	cut 2

PIECE
To make strip-pieced window unit, sew medium and dark strips together and cut into eight 1½″ wide units as shown. Remove the two bottom segments of units 14 and 16 as indicated by the two Xs in the illustration.

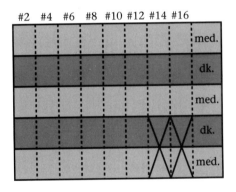

Make doors by folding 4½″ x 4½″ pieces, right sides together, to 2¼″ x 4½″. Sew each 2¼″ end, turn, and press. Assemble block, stitching strip-pieced window units to each other as indicated on diagram. Stitch doors into seams as indicated by stars on diagram, making sure that doors do not extend into the seam allowance on the top or bottom. Review construction of Fast Forty-Fives in *General Directions* (1a, 1b, etc.) for piecing roof. Stitch #21 to top of block.

APPLIQUE
Applique clouds above school, referring to whole quilt diagram for placement. See *General Directions, Applique,* for specific methods.

*Note: Stitch #21 to the top of the block

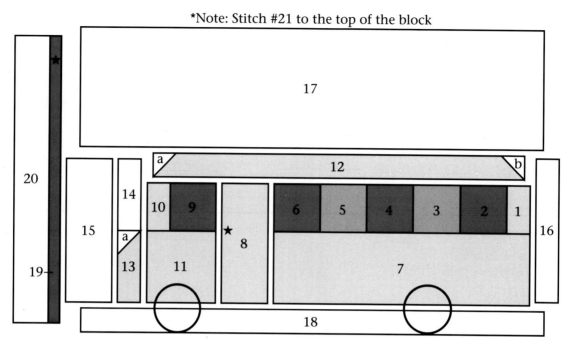

CUT

Fabric/Color	Pieces	Size or #
Background/ cream print #1	#12a, 12b, 13a	1½" x 1½"
	#14	1½" x 3½"
	#15	2½" x 6½"
	#16	1½" x 6½"
	#17	20½" x 5½"
	#18	20½" x 1½"
	#20	2" x 12½"
	#21*	22½" x 7½"
Bus/yellow stars	#1, 10	1½" x 2½"
	#7	11½" x 3½"
	#11	3½" x 3½"
	#12	16½" x 1½"
	#13	1½" x 3½"
Flagpole/speckled blk.	#19	1" x 12½"
Windows & door/ red-purple	#3, 5	2½" x 2½"
	#8	2½" x 5½"
Windows/blue-purple	#2, 4, 6, 9	2½" x 2½"
Applique Pieces (patterns on pages 125, 134)		
Wheels/cardboard	2" circle	cut 1
Clouds/freezer paper	#22, 23	trace 1 each
Sun/cardboard	5" circle	cut 1
Loose Inserts		
Doors	4½" x 5½"	cut 2
Flag	7½" x 3"	cut 1

PIECE

Make door by folding 4½" x 5½" piece, right sides together, to 2¼" x 5½". Sew each 2¼" end, turn, and press. Make flag by folding 7½" x 3" piece, right sides together, to 3¾" x 3". Stitch along both 3¾" sides, leaving 3" side open. Turn and press. Assemble block in units following diagram, stitching door and flag into seams indicated by stars on diagram. Review construction of Fast Forty-Fives in *General Directions* (1a, 1b, etc.). Stitch #21 to top of block.

APPLIQUE

Applique two wheels ¼" from bottom of block, referring to *General Directions, Applique,* for preparing circles. Applique clouds and sun above bus.

60

CUT

Fabric/Color	Pieces	Size or #
Background/ cream print #2	#1, 7, 10, 17	2½″ x 2½″
	#2a, 2b, 2c, 2d, 9a, 9b, 9c, 9d	1″ x 1″
	#3, 11	1″ x 4½″
	#5	2½″ x 1″
	#12	1½″ x 4½″
	#13	2½″ x 4½″
	#15, 19	3″ x 2½″
	#22	1½″ x 7½″
	#23	11½″ x 12½″
Desk/aqua	#14, 20	1½″ x 2½″
	#21	10½″ x 5½″
Chair/gold print	#4, 8	1″ x 4½″
	#6	2½″ x 2″
	#16, 18	1″ x 2½″
Apples/hot pink	#2, 9	2½″ x 2½″

Applique Pieces (patterns on pages 127, 134)

Clock/cardboard	5″ circle	cut 1
Hands/freezer paper	#24, 25	trace 1 each
Tips/freezer paper	#26	trace 2
Stem/freezer paper	#27	trace 2

PIECE

Assemble block in units following diagram. Review construction of Fast Forty-Fives in *General Directions* (1a, 1b, etc.).

APPLIQUE

Refer to *General Directions, Applique,* for preparing circles and for applique methods. Applique clock to #23. Applique hands to clock (fusible or freezer paper method). Applique stems onto apples.

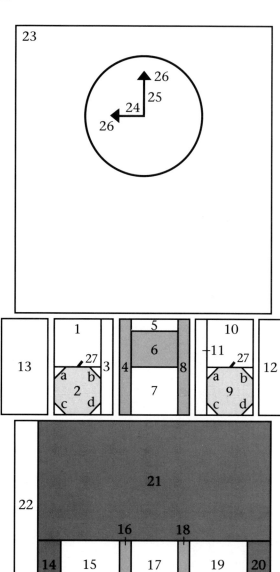

BLACKBOARD
Finished Size 25″ x 23″

CUT

Fabric/Color	Pieces	Size or #
Background/ cream print #2	#6	25½″ x 2½″
	#7	25½″ x 9½″
Blackboard/black print	#1	23½″ x 10½″
Blackbd. trim/purple	#2, 3	23½″ x 1½″
	#4, 5	1½″ x 12½″
Applique Pieces (patterns on pages 126-129)		
Arms/freezer paper	#8, 9, 15, 16	trace 1 each
Legs/freezer paper	#10, 11	trace 1 each
Neck/freezer paper	#17	trace 1
Shoes/freezer paper	#12, 18	trace 2 each
Girl's dress/freezer paper	#13	trace 1
Girl's hair/freezer paper	#14	trace 1
Boy's pants/freezer paper	#19, 20	trace 1 each
Boy's shirt/freezer paper	#21	trace 1
Boy's hair/freezer paper	#22	trace 1
Boy's pocket/freezer paper	#23	trace 1

PIECE
Assemble block following diagram.

APPLIQUE
Applique boy and girl, referring to *General Directions, Applique*. Pin or baste all pieces of children before appliqueing in place. Applique boy's pocket, leaving top open to insert optional handkerchief.

Continued on page 101.

TRIP TO THE ZOO

A day at the zoo is an adventure for young and old alike...third graders hold a buddy's hand as they exchange silly faces with baboons, mothers park toddlers in strollers to watch the lions pace, and Grandpa in his wheelchair laughs at an elephant blowing dirt. Each trip to the zoo is a unique experience.

Enjoy the little things. Someday you may look back and realize they were the big things. Country Magazine

SIZE: 36″ x 48″ (92 cm x 122 cm)

YARDAGE:
½ yd. (.5 m) tan solid for background
¼ yd. (.3 m) tan print for background
¼ yd. (.3 m) black for penguin and elephant ear
⅜ yd. (.4 m) gold dot for giraffe
⅜ yd. (.4 m) red for elephant
★ ⅜ yd. (.4 m) blue for split rail fence border
★ ⅜ yd. (.4 m) green for split rail fence border
★ ⅜ yd. (.4 m) gold for split rail fence border
★ ⅜ yd. (.4 m) red for split rail fence border
¼ yd. ¼″ grosgrain ribbon in 4 colors
⅔ yd. (.6 m) light brown for sashing
⅜ yd. (.4 m) binding
1½ yd. (1.4 m) backing
batting at least 40″ x 52″

Choose remainder of fabrics from your "stash". See *General Directions.* You will need ⅛ yd. pieces or less.

Applique, loose insert, and patchwork pattern pieces are on pages 131, 132. Circle patterns are on page 134.

★ Cut split rail fence strips first (see page 106.) Use remaining fence fabric for piecing.

For ease of piecing, some blocks have been simplified from the original quilt. Individual pull-apart drawings are accurate.

65

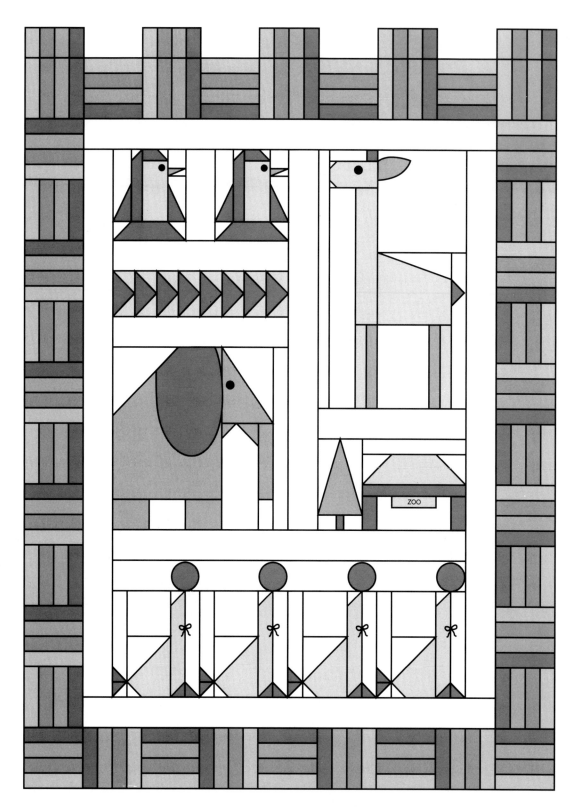

TRIP TO THE ZOO
Finished Size 36″ x 48″

Cutting chart is for one block only. **Make two blocks.**

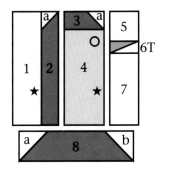

CUT

Fabric/Color	Pieces	Size or #
Bkgrnd./tan	#1	1¾″ x 5¼″
	#2a, 3a	1¼″ x 1¼″
	#5, 8a, 8b	1¾″ x 1¾″
	#6T	cut 1
	#7	1¾″ x 3½″
Body/black	#2	1¼″ x 5¼″
	#3	2¼″ x 1¼″
	#8	5½″ x 1¾″
Chest/cream	#4	2¼″ x 4½″
Beak/red	#6T	cut 1
Applique Piece (pattern on page 134)		
Eye/cardboard	½″ circle	cut 1
Loose Insert (pattern on page 131)		
Wing/freezer paper	wing	trace 2

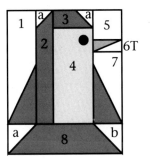

PIECE

Make two wings, referring to loose inserts section of *General Directions*. Template 6T is on page 131. Assemble two blocks in units following diagram, inserting wings in seams indicated by stars on diagram. Review construction of Fast Forty-Fives (1a, 1b, etc.) and templates in *General Directions*.

APPLIQUE

Applique eye or stitch on button. Refer to *General Directions, Applique,* for preparing circles.

CUT

Fabric/Color	Pieces	Size or #
Bkgrnd./tan	2″ x 3½″	cut 8
Loose Inserts		
Geese/prairie points	3½″ x 3½″	cut 8

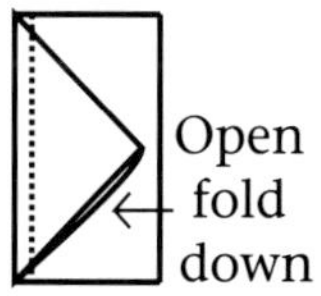

Open
fold
down

PIECE

Make 8 prairie points referring to prairie points directions in loose inserts section of *General Directions*. Baste a prairie point, inside the seam, to each background/tan piece, matching raw edges of prairie point to left edge of background piece. Sew the 8 units together, leaving the prairie points loose.

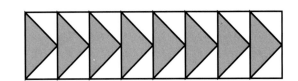

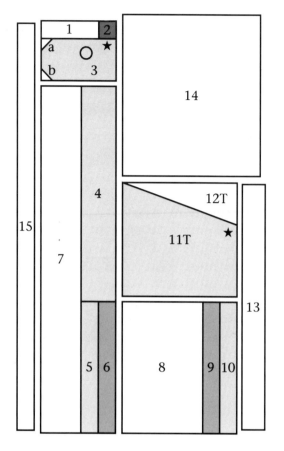

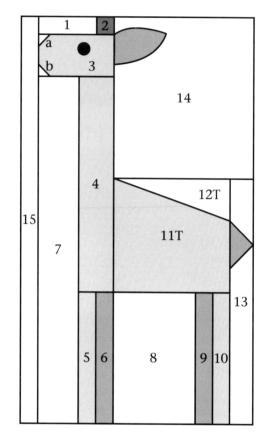

CUT

Fabric/Color	Pieces	Size or #
Bkgrnd./tan	#1	3″ x 1¼″
	#3a, 3b	1″ x 1″
	#7	2¼″ x 15″
	#8	4″ x 6″
	#12T	cut 1
	#13	1½″ x 10¾″
	#14	6½″ x 7¼″
	#15	1¼″ x 17½″
Body/gold dot	#3	3¾″ x 2¼″
	#4	2″ x 9½″
	#5, 10	1¼″ x 6″
	#11T	cut 1
Legs/dark gold	#6, 9	1¼″ x 6″
Horn/brown	#2	1¼″ x 1¼″
Applique Piece (pattern on page 134)		
Eye/cardboard	⅝″ circle	cut 1
Loose Inserts (pattern on page 131)		
Tail/prairie point	2″ x 2″	cut 1
Ear/freezer paper	ear	trace 1

PIECE

Make prairie point for tail, referring to prairie points directions in loose inserts section of *General Directions*. Make ear, referring to loose inserts section of *General Directions*. Templates 11T and 12T are on page 132. Assemble block in units following diagram, stitching tail and ear into seams indicated by stars on diagram. Review construction of Fast Forty-Fives (1a, 1b, etc.) and templates in *General Directions*.

APPLIQUE

Applique eye or stitch on a button. Refer to *General Directions, Applique*, for preparing circles.

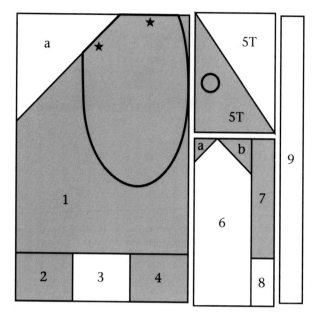

CUT

Fabric/Color	Pieces	Size or #
Bkgrnd./tan print	#1a	5″ x 5″
	#3	3″ x 2½″
	#5T	cut 1
	#6	3″ x 7½″
	#8	1½″ x 2½″
	#9	1½″ x 12½″
Body/red	#1	8″ x 10½″
	#2, 4	3″ x 2½″
	#5T	cut 1
	#6a	1½″ x 1½″
	#6b	2″ x 2″
	#7	1½″ x 5½″
Applique Piece (pattern on page 134)		
Eye/cardboard	¾″ circle	cut 1
Loose Insert (pattern on page 131)		
Ear/freezer paper	ear	trace 1

PIECE

Make ear, batting optional, referring to loose inserts section of *General Directions*. Template 5T is on page 131. Assemble block in units following diagram, stitching ear into seam indicated by star on diagram. Top edge of ear, also left open, will be caught in seam joining sashing strip to top of elephant block. Review construction of Fast Forty-Fives (1a, 1b, etc.) and templates in *General Directions*.

APPLIQUE

Applique eye or stitch on a button. Refer to *General Directions, Applique*, for preparing circles.

NINE-ELEPHANT QUILT - 42″ x 42″

Make 9 elephant blocks and sew together in rows of three, inserting braided tails (cut tails 3″ x 4½″ and refer to *General Directions, Loose Inserts*). Add one or two borders. A fat quarter will make two elephants, one yard will make all nine.

ZOO ENTRANCE

Finished Size 10″ x 6″

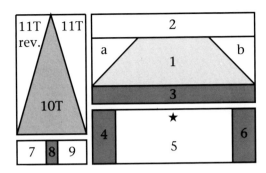

CUT

Fabric/Color	Pieces	Size or #
Bkgrnd./cream print	#1a, 1b	2½″ x 2½″
	#2	7½″ x 1½″
	#5	5½″ x 2¾″
	#11T, 11T rev.	cut 1 each
Roof/red	#1	7½″ x 2½″
Building & tree trunk/brown	#3	7½″ x 1¼″
	#4, 6	1½″ x 2¾″
	#8	1″ x 1½″
Tree/green	#10T	cut 1
Ground/gold	#7, 9	1¾″ x 1½″
Loose Insert		
Sign	3½″ x 2½″	cut 1

PIECE

To make sign, fold 3½″ x 2½″ rectangle, **right** sides together, to 3½″ x 1¼″. Stitch along short ends, turn, and press. Embroider or use permanent pen to add the word ZOO in the center. Templates 10T and 11T are on page 132. Assemble block in units following diagram, stitching raw edge of sign into seam indicated by star on diagram. Review construction of Fast Forty-Fives (1a, 1b, etc.) and templates in *General Directions*.

Continued on page 105.

SEEING IS BELIEVING

Christmas is anticipation...listening for bells and the pitter-patter of hooves on the roof...waiting to discover what Santa left in the stockings. Each family celebrates its own unique traditions, but the true Christmas message of love and hope is universal.

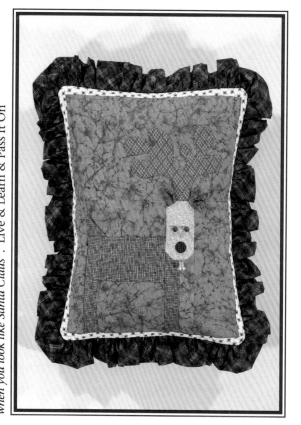

SIZE: 51″ x 51″ (132 cm x 132 cm)

YARDAGE:
1 yd. (1 m) navy blue star for background
½ yd. (.5 m) red plaid for house
¼ yd. (.3 m) white for snow & Santa trim
¼ yd. (.3 m) green for antlers
¼ yd. (.3 m) blue for sleigh
¼ yd. (.3 m) tan for window background
⅛ yd. (.2 m) black/tan plaid for inner border
1½ yd. (1.4 m) plaid for outer border
½ yd. (.5 m) binding
3¼ yds. (3 m) backing
batting at least 55″ x 55″
optional: 2 small brass bells for reindeer, ornaments
   for tree and door, red bead for holly

Choose the remainder of your fabrics from your "stash". See *General Directions*. You will need ⅛ yd. pieces or less, except for blue check for door (6″ x 12″ - 16 x 31 cm) and black for fireplace (6″ x 8″ - 16 x 21 cm).

Applique and loose insert pattern pieces are on page 133. Circle patterns are on page 134.

SEEING IS BELIEVING
Finished Size 51″ x 51″

Finished Size 42" x 5½"

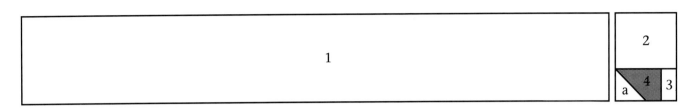

CUT

Fabric/Color	Pieces	Size or #
Background/navy stars	#1	38½" x 6"
	#2	4½" x 4"
	#3	1½" x 2½"
	#4a	2½" x 2½"
Sleigh/blue	#4	3½" x 2½"

PIECE

Assemble block in units following diagram. Review construction of Fast Forty-Fives in *General Directions* (1a, 1b, etc.).

FRONT OF SLEIGH

Finished Size 4" x 9½"

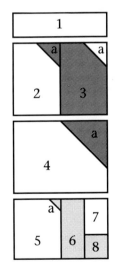

CUT

Fabric/Color	Pieces	Size or #
Background/navy stars	#1	4½" x 1½"
	#2	2½" x 3½"
	#3a	1½" x 1½"
	#4	4½" x 3½"
	#5	2½" x 3"
	#7	1½" x 2"
Sleigh/blue	#2a	1½" x 1½"
	#3	2½" x 3½"
	#4a	2½" x 2½"
Sled runners/dk. green	#5a	1" x 1"
	#6	1½" x 3"
	#8	1½" x 1½"

PIECE

Assemble block in units following diagram. Review construction of Fast Forty-Fives in *General Directions* (1a, 1b, etc.).

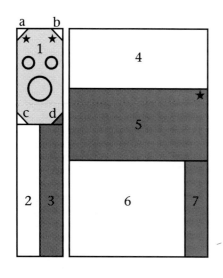

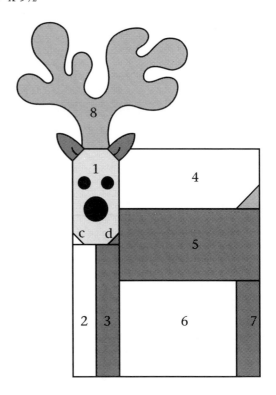

Cutting chart is for one block only. **Make two blocks.**

CUT

Fabric/Color	Pieces	Size or #
Background/navy stars	#1a, 1b, 1c	1″ x 1″
	#2	1½″ x 6″
	#4	6½″ x 3″
	#6	5½″ x 4½″
Reindeer body/brown	#1d	1″ x 1″
	#3	1½″ x 6″
	#5	6½″ x 3½″
	#7	1½″ x 4½″
Reindeer face/tan	#1	2½″ x 4½″
Applique Pieces (patterns on pages 133, 134)		
Nose/cardboard	1″ circle	cut 1
Eyes/cardboard	½″ circle	cut 1
Antlers/freezer paper	#8	trace 1
Loose Insert (pattern on page 133)		
Ears/freezer paper	ear	trace 2
Tail/8-layer prairie point	4″ x 4″	cut 1

PIECE

Review construction of Fast Forty-Fives, Loose Inserts, and prairie points in *General Directions*. Make tail by folding 4″ x 4″ square into eight-layer prairie point. Make two ears. Assemble two blocks in units following diagram, stitching tails and pleated ears into seams indicated by stars on diagram. Refer to *General Directions* for stitching loose inserts into Fast Forty-Fives.

APPLIQUE

Applique nose and eyes or stitch on buttons. Refer to *General Directions, Applique,* for preparing circles and other techniques. Applique antlers after top half of quilt has been sewn together (see *Quilt Top Assembly*, page 110).

SANTA

Finished Size 17″ x 13½″

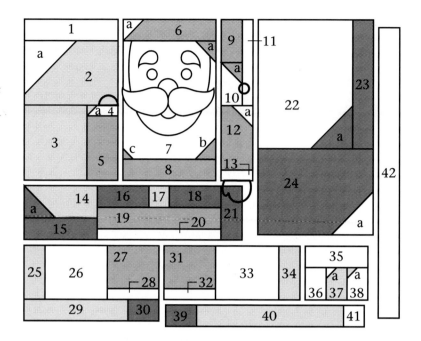

CUT

Fabric/Color	Pieces	Size or #
Background/navy stars	#1	5″ x 1½″
	#2a	3″ x 3″
	#6a, 12a, 41	1½″ x 1½″
	#10	1½″ x 2½″
	#11	1″ x 4½″
	#22	5″ x 6½″
	#24a	2½″ x 2½″
	#26, 33	3½″ x 3″
	#35	3½″ x 1½″
	#37a	1″ x 1″
	#36, 38	1½″ x 2″
	#42	1½″ x 14″
Santa body/red	#5, 12	2″ x 3½″
	#6, 8	5″ x 1½″
	#7a, 7b, 10a	1½″ x 1½″
	#7c	1″ x 1″
	#9	1½″ x 2½″
	#19	6½″ x 1½″
	#27, 31	3″ x 2½″
Sled/blue	#14a	2″ x 2″
	#15	4″ x 1½″
	#21	1½″ x 3″
	#22a	2½″ x 2½″
	#23	1½″ x 6½″
	#24	6″ x 4½″
Sled runners/dk. green	#25, 34	1½″ x 3″
	#29	5½″ x 1½″
	#37	1½″ x 2″
	#38a	1″ x 1″
	#40	7½″ x 1½″

Fabric/Color	Pieces	Size or #
Bag/tan & red stripe	#2	5″ x 3½″
	#3	3½″ x 4″
	#4a	1″ x 1″
	#14	4″ x 2″
Santa fur trim, beard/white	#4, 13	2″ x 1″
	#7	5″ x 6″
	#20	6½″ x 1″
	#28, 32	3″ x 1″
Belt buckle/gold	#17	1½″ x 1½″
Belt, boots/black	#16, 18	3″ x 1½″
	#30, 39	2″ x 1½″

Applique Pieces (patterns on pages 133, 134)

Face/freezer paper	#43	trace 1
Nose/cardboard	1″ circle	cut 1
Mouth/freezer paper	#44	trace 1
Mustache/freezer paper	#45	trace 1, trace 1 rev.
Eyes/cardboard	⅝″ circle	cut 1
Eyebrows/freezer paper	#46	trace 1, trace 1 reversed
Mittens/freezer paper	#47, 48	trace 1 each
Hat tassle/cardboard	¾″ circle	cut 1

PIECE

Assemble block in units following diagram. Review construction of Fast Forty-Fives in *General Directions*.

APPLIQUE

Applique face and mittens, referring to *General Directions, Applique.* Overlap nose and mouth with mustache. Buttons can be substituted for applique eyes.

78

LEFT ROOF

Finished Size 28½" x 6½"

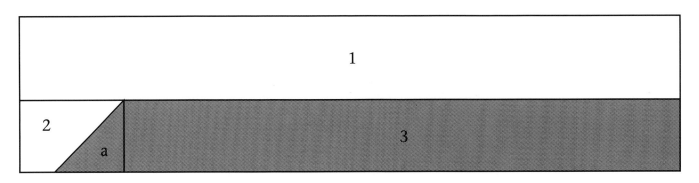

CUT

Fabric/Color	Pieces	Size or #
Background/navy stars	#1	29" x 4"
	#2	5" x 3½"
Roof/brown check	#2a	3½" x 3½"
	#3	24½" x 3½"

PIECE

Assemble block in units following diagram. Review construction of Fast Forty-Fives in *General Directions* (1a, 1b, etc.).

RIGHT ROOF

Finished Size 13½" x 6½"

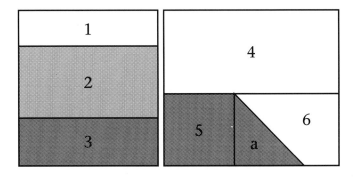

CUT

Fabric/Color	Pieces	Size or #
Background/navy stars	#1	6½" x 2"
	#4	8" x 4"
	#6	5" x 3½"
Roof/brown check	#3	6½" x 2½"
	#5, 6a	3½" x 3½"
Chimney/Christmas plaid	#2	6½" x 3½"

PIECE

Assemble block in units following diagram. Review construction of Fast Forty-Fives in *General Directions* (1a, 1b, etc.).

Continued on page 108.

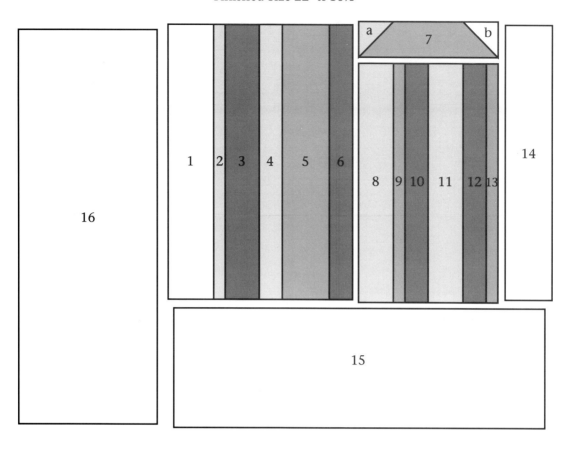

CUT

Fabric/Color	Pieces	Size or #
Background/blue	#1, 14	2½″ x 12″
	#7b	2″ x 2″
	#15	16½″ x 5½″
	#16	6½″ x 17″
Booster tail/lt. blue	#7	6½″ x 2″
Fire/4-6 warm colors	#2	1″ x 12″
	#3	2″ x 12″
	#4, 6	1½″ x 12″
	#5	2½″ x 12″
	#8	2″ x 10½″
	#7a (same color as 8)	2″ x 2″
	#9	1″ x 10½″
	#10	1½″ x 10½″
	#11	2″ x 10½″
	#12	1½″ x 10½″
	#13	1″ x 10½″

Applique Pieces (patterns on pages 114-117)

Fire clouds/freezer paper	#17, 18, 19, 20	trace 1 each
Earth/freezer paper	#21 + 22	trace 1 from joined pattern pieces

PIECE

Assemble block in units following diagram. Review construction of Fast Forty-Fives in *General Directions* (1a, 1b, etc.).

APPLIQUE

Applique clouds in numerical order. Applique Earth. **Hint:** Cut freezer paper 5″ x 20″. With a yardstick, draw a straight line along the bottom. Using this line to match the bottom edges of the Earth patterns, trace #21 + 22 to make the Earth template. See diagram on page 81 for applique placement.

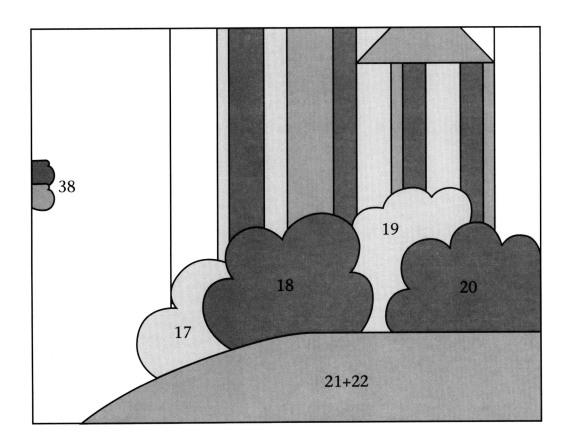

38

19

18

17

20

21+22

Quilt Top Assembly

ASSEMBLE BLOCKS
Stitch blocks together as shown in the *Quilt Top Assembly Diagram*, page 82. This unit should now measure 32½" x 49½". Applique the hands to the ends of the astronaut's arms.

CUT BORDERS
Rose Border Insert
The narrow inside rose border is a ¼" loose insert which **does not** increase the size of the quilt. Cut 5 strips 1" x 45" (or across the width of the fabric. Trim two of these strips to 1" x 32½". Cut the third strip in half and sew one of the halves to each of the 1" x 45" strips, using a diagonal seam as described in the binding section of *General Directions*. Trim these strips to 1" x 49½".

Navy Outside Border and Binding
Cut these strips from the length of the fabric.
    Two strips 4½" x 49½" for the side borders
    Two strips 4½" x 40½" for the top and bottom borders
    Four strips 2¼" x 63" for the binding

ATTACH BORDERS
Rose Inserted Border
Fold and press the rose strips of fabric **wrong** sides together so they are now ½" wide. Pin these folded strips to the right and left sides of the quilt, matching the raw edges. Baste in place ⅛" in from the raw edge. Repeat the above procedure for the top and bottom. The inserts will overlap each other on the ends.

Navy Outside Border
Lay a 4½" x 49½" navy border, **right** side down on the left side of the quilt. The rose inserted border should be sandwiched between the quilt top and the navy border, but it will remain loose. Stitch in place. Repeat for the right side of the quilt. Press only the navy border toward the outside edge of the quilt. Sew the 4½" x 40½" strips to the top and bottom of the quilt in the same manner.

FINISH
See *General Directions* for layering, basting, quilting and binding suggestions.

81

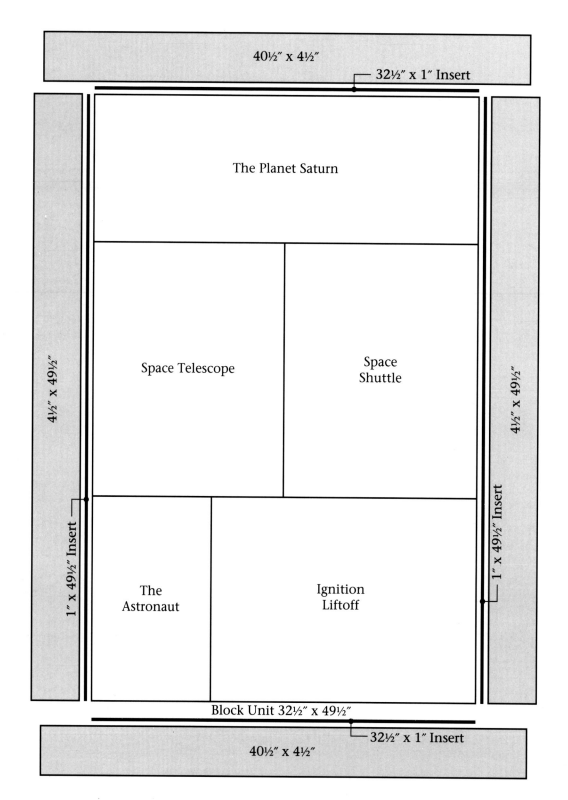

40½" x 4½"

32½" x 1" Insert

The Planet Saturn

Space Telescope

Space
Shuttle

4½" x 49½"

4½" x 49½"

1" x 49½" Insert

1" x 49½" Insert

The
Astronaut

Ignition
Liftoff

Block Unit 32½" x 49½"

32½" x 1" Insert

40½" x 4½"

SHOOT FOR THE STARS
QUILT TOP ASSEMBLY DIAGRAM
Dimensions include seam allowance.

COCK-A-DOODLE-DOO...
Finished Size 9″ x 11″

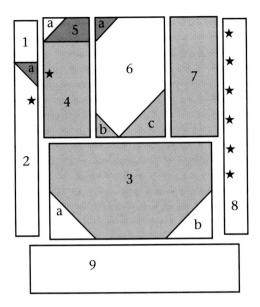

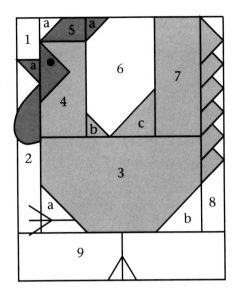

CUT

Fabric/Color	Pieces	Size or #
Bkgrnd./cream solid	#1	1½″ x 2¼″
	#2	1½″ x 7¾″
	#3a, 3b	2½″ x 2½″
	#5a	1½″ x 1½″
	#6	3½″ x 5½″
	#8	1½″ x 9½″
	#9	9½″ x 2½″
Body/blue	#3	7½″ x 4½″
	#4	2½″ x 4½″
	#6b	1½″ x 1½″
	#6c	2½″ x 2½″
	#7	2½″ x 5½″
Comb & beak/red	#2a, 6a	1½″ x 1½″
	#5	2½″ x 1½″

Loose Inserts (pattern on page 118)

Face/prairie point	2½″ x 2½″	cut 1
Wattle/freezer paper	wattle	trace 1
Tail/prairie points	2½″ x 2½″	cut 6

PIECE

Review construction of Fast Forty-Fives in *General Directions* (1a, 1b, etc.). Make prairie point for face, referring to prairie point directions in loose inserts section of *General Directions*.

Make wattle, referring to loose inserts section of *General Directions*.

For tail, make 6 prairie points. To place first prairie point, match raw edge of #8 and raw edges of prairie point 2″ from bottom corner of #8. Place next prairie point inside previous prairie point, moving up in 1″ increments. Continue until you have placed all six prairie points. Machine baste just inside the seam allowance. Assemble block in units following diagram, stitching face and wattle into seams indicated by stars on diagram.

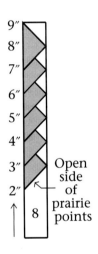

Machine or hand embroider feet. Embroider an eye or sew on a button through "face" (loose insert prairie point).

ASSEMBLE ROW

Stitch chicks unit between hen and rooster. New unit should measure 11½″ x 21½″.

CUT

Fabric/Color	Pieces	Size or #
Bkgrnd./cream print	#1	8″ x 4″
	#2	5″ x 3″
	#3	3½″ x 3″
	#4T	cut 1
	#6T	cut 1
	#7a, 7b	1¾″ x 1¾″
	#9a	2″ x 2″
Barn/red & black check	#2a, 3a	3″ x 3″
	#4T	cut 1
	#4T reversed	cut 1
	#9	9½″ x 3″
	#10, 12	3½″ x 4″
Silo/blue	#8	3″ x 7¼″
	#9b	2″ x 2″
	#13	1½″ x 6½″
Window, silo top, door opening/black	#5	2½″ x 2½″
	#7	3″ x 1¾″
	#11	3½″ x 4″
Loose Inserts		
Barn doors	4½″ x 4″	cut 2

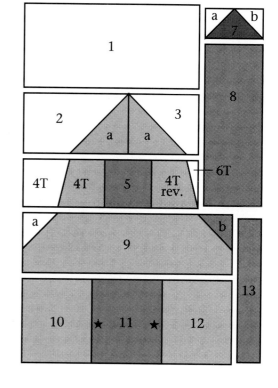

PIECE

Review construction of Fast Forty-Fives in *General Directions* (1a, 1b, etc.). See *General Directions* for loose inserts and use of templates (templates are on page 118) . To make one door, fold 4″ x 4½″ rectangle into a rectangle 2¼″ x 4″, **wrong** sides together. Stitch across top and bottom. Turn, press, repeat for other door. Assemble block in units following diagram, stitching doors into seams indicated by stars on diagram. The doors should not extend into the ¼″ seam allowances.

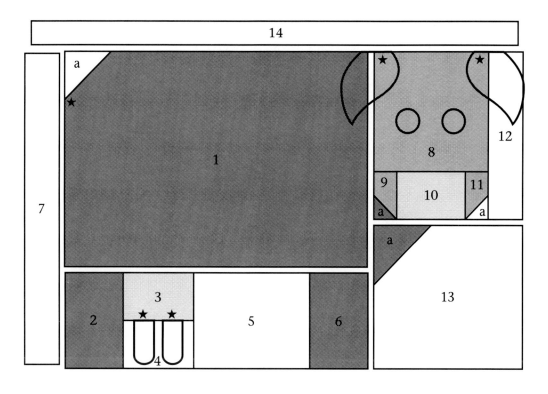

CUT

Fabric/Color	Pieces	Size or #
Bkgrnd./solid cream	#1a	2½″ x 2½″
	#4	3½″ x 2½″
	#5	5½″ x 4½″
	#7	2″ x 13½″
	#11a	1½″ x 1½″
	#12	2″ x 7½″
	#13	7″ x 6½″
	#14	21½″ x 1½″
Cow/plaid	#1	13½″ x 9½″
	#2, 6	3″ x 4½″
	#9a	1½″ x 1½″
	#13a	3″ x 3″
Face/green	#8	5½″ x 5½″
	#9, 11	1½″ x 2½″
Nose/light pink	#10	3½″ x 2½″
Udder/dark pink	#3	3½″ x 2½″
Applique Piece (pattern on page 134)		
Eyes/cardboard	1″ circle	cut 1
Loose Inserts (patterns on page 118)		
Ears/freezer paper	ear	trace 2
Milkers/freezer paper	milker	trace 2
Tail/braid	9″ x 3″	cut 1

PIECE

Review construction of Fast Forty-Fives in *General Directions* (1a, 1b, etc.). Make two ears and two milkers referring to loose inserts section of *General Directions*. Make braided tail referring to braids part of loose inserts section of *General Directions*. Assemble block in units following diagram, stitching ears (facing in), milkers, and tail into seams indicated by stars on diagram.

APPLIQUE

Applique eyes or stitch on buttons. Refer to *General Directions, Applique*, for preparing circles.

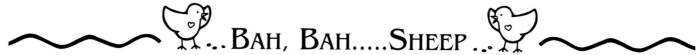

...Bah, Bah.....Sheep...

Finished Size 10″ x 9″

CUT

Fabric/Color	Pieces	Size or #
Bkgrnd./blue	#1a, 1b	2½″ x 2½″
	#5, 10	2½″ x 3½″
	#8	2½″ x 1½″
	#11, 12	1½″ x 9½″
Body/tan stripe	#1	8½″ x 2½″
	#2, 4	3¼″ x 4½″
	#5a, 10a	2½″ x 2½″
	#6	4½″ x 2½″
Face/black	#3	3″ x 4½″
Feet/plaid	#7, 9	1½″ x 1½″
Applique Piece (pattern on page 134)		
Eyes/cardboard	½″ circle	cut 1
Loose Insert (pattern on page 118)		
Ears/freezer paper	ear	trace 2

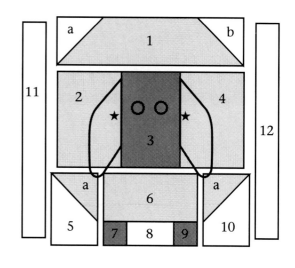

PIECE

Review construction of Fast Forty-Fives in *General Directions* (1a, 1b, etc.). Make two ears, batting optional, referring to loose inserts section of *General Directions*. Assemble block in units following diagram, stitching ears, facing opposite directions, into seams indicated by stars on diagram.

APPLIQUE

Applique two eyes or stitch on buttons. Refer to *General Directions, Applique,* for preparing circles.

...Cornstalks...

Finished Size 3″ x 9″

Cutting chart is for one block only. **Make three blocks.**

CUT

Fabric/Color	Pieces	Size or #
Bkgrnd./cream print	#1T, 3T, 5T	cut 1 each
Cornstalk/green	#2T	cut 1
Leaf/green print	#4T	cut 1

PIECE

This block is made from templates which are found on page 119. See directions for templates in *General Directions*. Assemble three blocks in units following diagram.

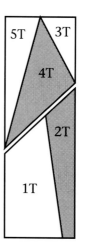

TRACTOR
Finished Size 15″ x 9″

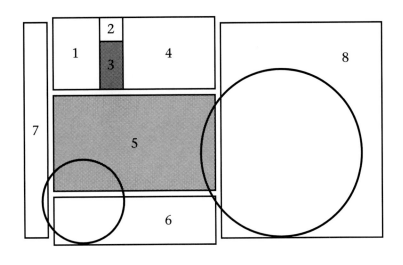

CUT

Fabric/Color	Pieces	Size or #
Bkgrnd./cream print	#1	2½″ x 3½″
	#2	1½″ x 1½″
	#4	4½″ x 3½″
	#6	7½″ x 2½″
	#7	1½″ x 9½″
	#8	7½″ x 9½″
Body/red	#5	7½″ x 4½″
Smokestack/blue	#3	1½″ x 2½″
Applique Pieces (patterns on page 134)		
Wheels/cardboard	7″ circle	cut 1
	3½″ circle	cut 1

PIECE
Assemble block in units following diagram.

APPLIQUE
Applique wheels ¼″ from raw edge of block to allow for seam allowance. Refer to *General Directions, Applique,* for preparing circles.

WAGON
Finished Size 9″ x 9″

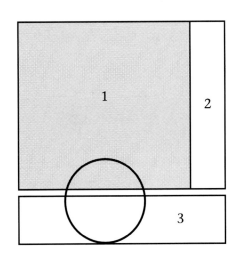

CUT

Fabric/Color	Pieces	Size or #
Bkgrnd./cream print	#2	2″ x 7½″
	#3	9½″ x 2½″
Wagon/plaid	#1	8″ x 7½″
Applique Piece (pattern on page 134)		
Wheel/cardboard	3½″ circle	cut 1

PIECE
Assemble block following diagram.

APPLIQUE
Applique wheels ¼″ from raw edge of block to allow for seam allowance. Refer to *General Directions, Applique,* for preparing circles.

ASSEMBLE ROW
Sew three corn blocks, and tractor and wagon blocks together referring to *Quilt Top Assembly Diagram,* page 89. Unit should measure 33½″ x 9½″. Embroider a hitch between the wagon and the tractor.

CUT SASHING

Cut three strips 21½" x 2½" of green border fabric
Cut three strips 10½" x 2½" of green border fabric
Cut one strip 2½" x 39½" of green border fabric

ASSEMBLE BLOCKS & SASHING

Stitch blocks together with sashing, referring to *Quilt Top Assembly Diagram.*

CUT FENCE BORDER

Cut four strips 1½" x 45" of brown fence fabric
Cut five strips 2" x 45" of brown fence fabric
Cut six strips 1½" x 45" of green border fabric
Cut four strips 3" x 24" of green border fabric
Cut four strips 3" x 29½" of green border fabric
Cut four pieces 15" x 10½" of green border fabric
Cut four pieces 20" x 10½" of green border fabric

ASSEMBLE FENCE RAILS

Sew two units as shown using 1½" x 45" brown and green strips. Press seams in one direction. Square up. Cut into eighteen 4½" lengths.

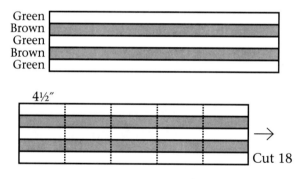

From the five 2" x 45" strips, cut twenty-two 5½" fence posts and twenty-two 2" squares for modified prairie point fence post tops. To press prairie points, refer to prairie points directions in loose inserts section of *General Directions*. Set aside.
Sew four fence rails and five posts together as shown. Make two sets. Sew five fence rail units and six posts together. Make two sets.

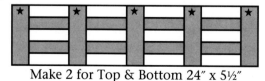

Make 2 for Top & Bottom 24" x 5½"

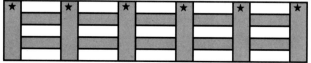

Make 2 for Sides 29½" x 5½"

Pin a prairie point to the top of each fence post, right sides together, raw edges even. Machine baste inside the ¼" seam allowance.

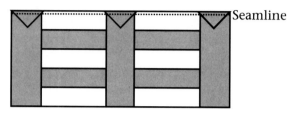

Seamline

Stitch a 3" x 24" strip to the top of each five-post unit, sandwiching the prairie points. Sew the other 3" x 24" strips to the bottom of each five-post unit. Repeat with the six-post units, using the 3" x 29½" strips. Sew a 15" x 10½" piece to each end of the five-post units, and sew a 20" x 10½" piece to each end of the six-post units.

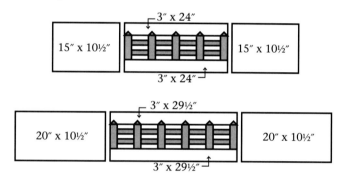

ATTACH BORDER

Fold the top center of the pieced block unit and one of the five-post border units in half to find the center points. With **right** sides together, match center points and pin border to pieced block unit. (Side fence posts face out for a wall quilt and in for a bed quilt.) Start and stop sewing ¼" from the sides of the quilt. Sew bottom border on in the same manner. The ends of the borders will extend beyond the quilt for mitering. In the same manner, sew side borders with six-post units to sides of quilt, starting and stopping ¼" in from the edges of the quilt. Press seam allowances to the outside.
To miter the corners, lay the quilt **right** side up on the ironing board. Overlap one border onto the other and fold one border under to a 45° angle, matching the corners. Press. Pin in place. Applique along fold from the right side, beginning at the inner corner and sewing to the outside edge of the quilt. Trim excess fabric ¼" from seamline.

FINISH

See *General Directions* for layering, basting, quilting, and binding suggestions.

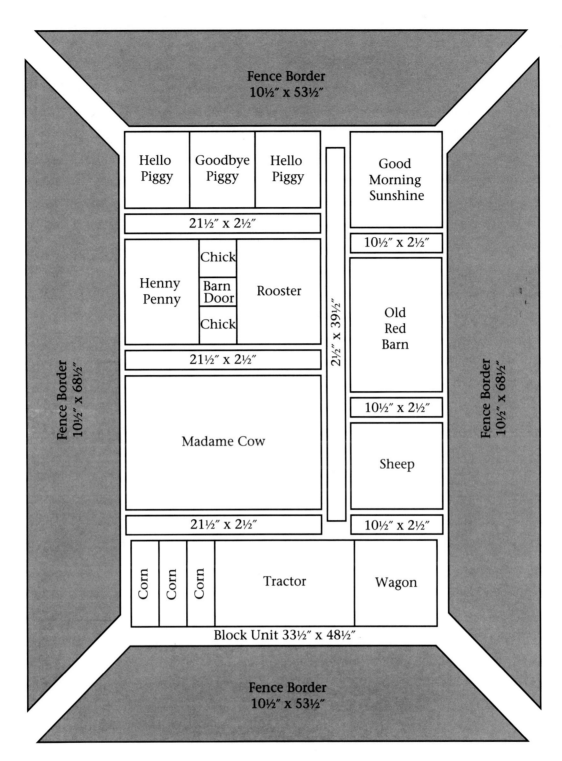

Fence Border
10½" x 53½"

Fence Border
10½" x 68½"

Hello Piggy | Goodbye Piggy | Hello Piggy

21½" x 2½"

Good Morning Sunshine

10½" x 2½"

Henny Penny | Chick / Barn Door / Chick | Rooster

21½" x 2½"

2½" x 39½"

Old Red Barn

10½" x 2½"

Madame Cow

Sheep

21½" x 2½"

10½" x 2½"

Corn Corn Corn | Tractor | Wagon

Block Unit 33½" x 48½"

Fence Border
10½" x 68½"

Fence Border
10½" x 53½"

E-I-E-I-O
QUILT TOP ASSEMBLY DIAGRAM
Dimensions include seam allowance.

DUMP TRUCK

Finished Size 19″ x 9″

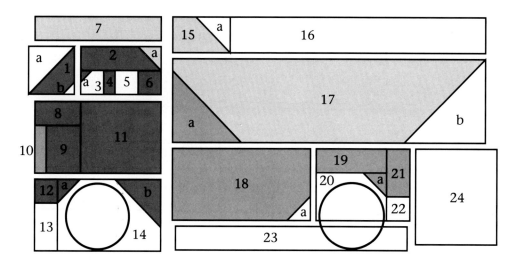

Cutting chart is for sashing and one block only.
Make two blocks.

CUT (*cut first)

Fabric/Color	Piece or #	Size or #
Bkgrnd./lt. teal check (sashing)	*cut 1	43″ x 4½″
	cut 2	1½″ x 9½″
	cut 1	3″ x 9½″
Bkgrnd./lt. teal check (block)	#1a	2½″ x 2½″
	#13	1½″ x 2½″
	#14	5″ x 3½″
	#15a	2″ x 2″
	#16	11½″ x 2″
	#17b	4″ x 4″
	#18a, 22	1½″ x 1½″
	#20	3½″ x 2½″
	#23	10½″ x 1½″
	#24	4″ x 4½″
Truck cab/dk. teal plaid	#1, 14b	2½″ x 2½″
	#2	4″ x 1½″
	#3a	1″ x 1″
	#4	1″ x 1½″
	#6, 12, 14a	1½″ x 1½″
	#8	2½″ x 1½″
	#9	2″ x 2½″
	#11	4″ x 3½″
Truck box/med. teal	#2a	1½″ x 1½″
	#7	6″ x 1½″
	#15	3″ x 2″
	#17	14″ x 4″
Truck bed/ dark teal	#17a	3½″ x 3½″
	#18	6½″ x 3½″
	#19	3½″ x 1½″
	#20a	1½″ x 1½″
	#21	1½″ x 2½″

Windows/cream	#1b	1″ x 1″
	#3, 5	1½″ x 1½″
Truck grill/teal	#10	1″ x 2½″
Applique Pieces (pattern on page 134)		
Wheels/cardboard	2¾″ circle	cut 1

PIECE

Assemble two blocks in units following diagram.
Review construction of Fast Forty-Fives in *General Directions* (1a, 1b, etc.).

ASSEMBLE ROW

Sew row as shown. Sew 43″ x 4½″ strip to top of row.

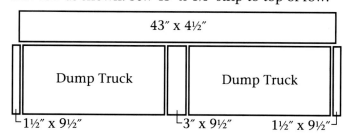

APPLIQUE

Refer to *General Directions, Applique*, for preparing circles. Applique wheels ¼″ from the raw edge at the bottom of the block to allow for the seam allowance.

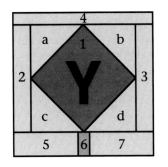

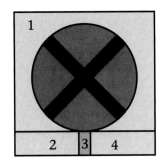

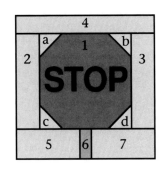

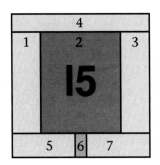

CUT FOR YIELD SIGN

Fabric/Color	Pieces	Size or #
Bkgrnd./blue check border fabric	#1a, 1b, 1c, 1d	2¾″ x 2¾″
	#2, 3	1¼″ x 5″
	#4	6½″ x 1″
	#5, 7	3¼″ x 1½″
Yield sign/tan ck.	#1	5″ x 5″
Signpost/gold	#6	1″ x 1½″
Applique Piece (pattern on page 120)		
"Y"/fusible web		trace 1

CUT FOR RAILROAD CROSSING SIGN

Fabric/Color	Pieces	Size or #
Bkgrnd./blue check border fabric	#1	6½″ x 5½″
	#2, 4	3¼″ x 1½″
Signpost/gold	#3	1″ x 1½″
Applique Pieces (pattern on page 134)		
Circle/cardboard	4½″ circle	cut 1
Railroad "X"/fusible web	1½″ x 5″	trace 2

CUT FOR STOP SIGN

Fabric/Color	Pieces	Size or #
Bkgrnd./blue check border fabric	#1a, 1b, 1c, 1d	1½″ x 1½″
	#2, 3	1½″ x 4½″
	#4	6½″ x 1¼″
	#5, 7	3¼″ x 1¾″
Stop sign/red check	#1	4½″ x 4½″
Signpost/gold	#6	1″ x 1¾″
Applique Pieces (pattern on page 120)		
Letters/fusible web		trace 1 set

CUT FOR SPEED SIGN

Fabric/Color	Pieces	Size or #
Bkgrnd./blue check border fabric	#1, 3	1¾″ x 4¾″
	#4	6½″ x 1¼″
	#5, 7	3¼″ x 1½″
Speed sign/blue check	#2	4″ x 4¾″
Signpost/gold	#6	1″ x 1½″
Applique Pieces (pattern on page 120)		
"15"/fusible web		trace 1 set

PIECE

Piece each block in order labeled in diagrams. Review construction of Fast Forty-Fives in *General Directions* (1a, 1b, etc.).

APPLIQUE

Applique Railroad Crossing circle referring to *General Directions, Applique* for preparing circles and other techniques. Use fusible web to apply "X".

Trace letters, in reverse, onto web. Fuse web to black fabric, cut shapes out on drawn lines (do not add seam allowance). Stitch around fused design with zigzag or buttonhole stitch.

TO MAKE LARGE PILLOWS:

Finished size 12″ x 12″

To cut pieces for large sign pillows, subtract ½″ seam allowance from each patchwork piece measurement. Double the measurement and then add back the ½″ seam allowance.

For example, for Yield Sign #1a:

    2¾″ minus ½″ equals 2¼″
    2¼″ doubled equals 4½″
    4½″ plus ½″ equals 5″
    piece #1a for pillow is cut 5″ x 5″

Continue for all pieces. Double the size of the circle for the Railroad Crossing and double the size of all the lettering.

ASSEMBLE ROWS

Sew rows of cars and trucks to each other as shown in the *Quilt Top Assembly Diagram*. This unit should now measure 43" x 51½".

Cut teal check borders as follows:

Two 6½" x 51½" for the sides

Two 43" x 6½" for the top and bottom

Stitch the 6½" x 51½" borders to the sides of the quilt. Stitch one road sign to each end of the remaining two 43" x 6½" borders. Sew these to the top and bottom of the quilt. Make sure the seam where the road sign was sewn to the border strip matches to the seam where the side border was sewn onto the quilt. Piece backing horizontally. Refer to *General Directions, Finishing*.

FINISH

See *General Directions* for layering, basting, quilting, and binding suggestions.

Stop Sign	43" x 6½"	Railroad Crossing
6½" x 51½"	Tow Trucks & Sashing	6½" x 51½"
	Fire Engines & Sashing	
	Police Cars & Sashing	
	Ambulances & Sashing	
	Dump Trucks & Sashing	
	Block Unit 43" x 51½"	
Speed Sign	43" x 6½"	Yield Sign

WHEELS & MORE WHEELS

QUILT TOP ASSEMBLY DIAGRAM

Dimensions include seam allowance.

TEN GALLON HAT

Finished Size 11″ x 14″

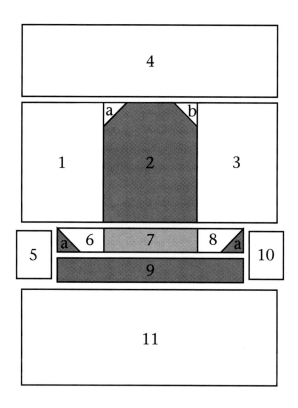

Cutting chart is for one block only. **Make two blocks.**

CUT

Fabric/Color	Pieces	Size or #
Bkgrnd./tan	#1, 3	4″ x 5½″
	#2a, 2b	1½″ x 1½″
	#4	11½″ x 3½″
	#5, 10	2″ x 2½″
	#6, 8	2½″ x 1½″
	#11	11½″ x 4½″
Hat/dk. brown	#2	4½″ x 5½″
	#6a, 8a	1½″ x 1½″
	#9	8½″ x 1½″
Hatband/plaid	#7	4½″ x 1½″

PIECE

Assemble two blocks in units following diagram. Review construction of Fast Forty-Fives in *General Directions* (1a, 1b, etc.). **Note:** These two blocks will be sewn on the right and left side of the two saddles to complete the row.

93

WESTERN SADDLE
Finished Size 8″ x 14″

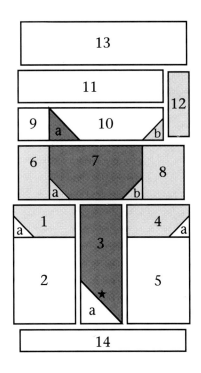

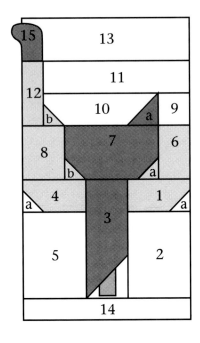

Cutting chart is for one block only. **Make two blocks, one in reverse.**

CUT (*cut first)

Fabric/Color	Piece or #	Size or #
Bkgrnd./tan (sashing)	*cut 1	2½″ x 14½″
Bkgrnd./tan	#1a, 4a	1½″ x 1½″
	#2, 5	3½″ x 4½″
	#3a	2½″ x 2½″
	#9	2″ x 2″
	#10	6″ x 2″
	#11	7½″ x 2″
	#13	8½″ x 2½″
	#14	8½″ x 1½″
Leg strap/dk. brown	#3	2½″ x 6″
Seat/blue	#7	5″ x 3″
	#10a	2″ x 2″
Saddle/med. brown	#1, 4	3½″ x 2″
	#6	2″ x 3″
	#7a, 7b, 10b	1½″ x 1½″
	#8	2½″ x 3″
	#12	1½″ x 3½″
Applique Piece (pattern on page 121)		
Horn/freezer paper	#15	trace 1
Loose Insert		
Stirrup/plaid	2½″ x 5″	cut 1

PIECE

Assemble one block in units following diagram, inserting stirrup as shown. Make one block in reverse. Review construction of Fast Forty-Fives in *General Directions* (1a, 1b, etc.).

To make stirrup, fold 2½″ x 5″ stirrup **right** sides together to 1¼″ x 5″. Stitch along 5″ side and turn right side out. Match raw edges to form loop. For saddle facing right, lay #3a, open, on bottom of #3. Pin-mark along top of #3a, remove. Center stirrup horizontally in marked square, matching fold to right edge of #3. Lay #3a on top with fold running from upper left to lower right. Stitch, trim, open, and press. For saddle facing left, repeat above but place fold of stirrup on left of #3 and sew diagonally from upper right to lower left.

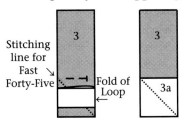

ASSEMBLE ROW

Assemble the row of hats and saddles as shown. Row should measure 40½″ x 14½″.

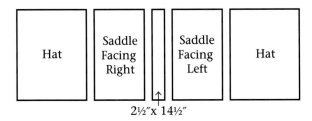

APPLIQUE

Applique saddle horns after assembling row. Reverse horn on second block. Refer to *General Directions, Applique.*

ASSEMBLE ROWS
Sew rows together by referring to *Quilt Top Assembly Diagram*. Unit should measure 40½" x 52½".

CUT AND ATTACH BORDERS
From the teal border fabric, cut four strips 6½" x 52½". Sew the side borders on first, then the top and bottom borders.

FINISH
See *General Directions* for layering, basting, quilting, and binding suggestions.

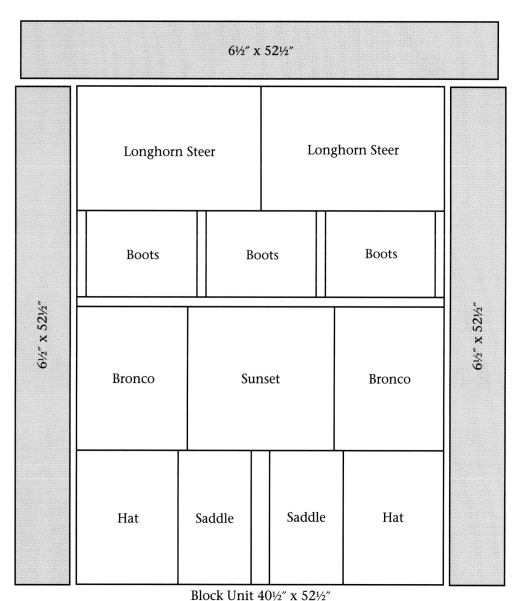

A COWBOY NEEDS A QUILT
QUILT TOP ASSEMBLY DIAGRAM
Dimensions include seam allowance.

CIRCUS CAGE
Finished Size 12″ x 10″

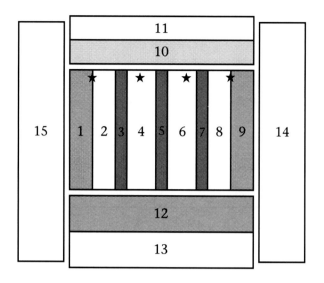

CUT

Fabric/Color	Pieces	Size or #
Background/tan	#2, 8	1½″ x 5½″
	#4, 6	1¾″ x 5½″
	#11	8½″ x 1½″
	#13	8½″ x 2″
	#14, 15	2½″ x 10½″
Cage/blue check	#1, 9	1½″ x 5½″
	#12	8½″ x 2″
Bars/navy solid	#3, 5, 7	1″ x 5½″
Cage top/red	#10	8½″ x 1½″
Loose Insert (pattern on page 123)		
Cage scallops/freezer paper	scallop	trace 4
Applique Piece (pattern on page 134)		
Wheels/cardboard	2½″ circle	cut 1

PIECE

Make four scallops referring to loose inserts section of *General Directions*. Assemble block in units following diagram, stitching the four scallops into seam indicated by stars in diagram. Place the two end scallops ¼″ in from raw edges of unit.

APPLIQUE

After block has been pieced, applique two wheels ½″ from bottom edge of block. Refer to *General Directions, Applique,* for preparing circles.

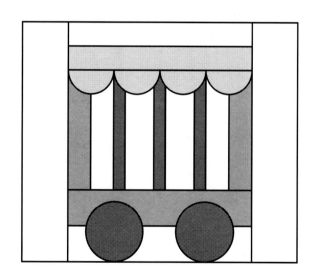

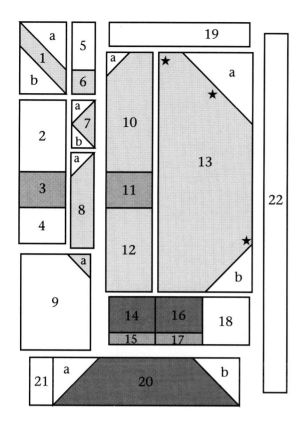

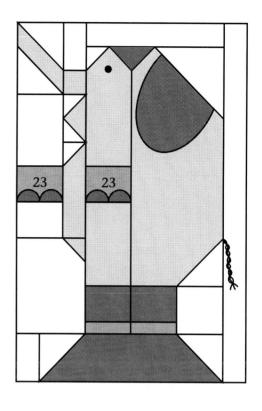

Cutting chart is for one block only. **Make three blocks, each with a different fabric for the body.**

CUT

Fabric/Color	Pieces	Size or #
Background/tan	#1a, 1b, 13b, 18, 20a, 20b	2½″ x 2½″
	#2	2½″ x 3½″
	#4	2½″ x 2″
	#5, 21	1½″ x 2½″
	#7a, 7b, 8a, 10a	1½″ x 1½″
	#9	3½″ x 4½″
	#13a	3½″ x 3½″
	#19	6½″ x 1½″
	#22	1½″ x 15½″
Body/check	#1	2½″ x 3½″
	#6, 9a	1½″ x 1½″
	#7	1½″ x 2½″
	#8	1½″ x 4½″
	#10	2½″ x 5½″
	#12	2½″ x 4″
	#13	4½″ x 10½″
Front feet/putty	#3, 11	2½″ x 2″
Back feet/brown	#15, 17	2½″ x 1″
Legs/black	#14, 16	2½″ x 2″
Platform/black stars	#20	8½″ x 2½″

Applique Pieces (patterns on pages 123, 134)

Toenails/freezer paper	#23	trace 4
Eye/cardboard	⅝″ circle	cut 1
Loose Inserts (pattern on page 124)		
Tail/braid	2½″ x 7″	cut 1
Hat/mod. prairie point	2½″ x 2½″	cut 1
Ear/freezer paper	ear	trace 1

PIECE

Make three blocks in units, each with a different fabric for the body. See *General Directions* for Fast Forty-Fives (1a, 1b, etc.). Make modified prairie point hat, ear, and braided tail, referring to *General Directions, Loose Inserts*. Stitch tail, hat, and ear into seams indicated by stars in diagram.

APPLIQUE

After each block has been pieced, applique toenails and eye (or sew on a button). Refer to *General Directions, Applique,* for preparing circles.

Rows of Star Blocks

Finished Size of One Block 3″

CUT FOR QUICK-PIECING 18 STARS

(6 red, 6 purple, and 6 turquoise stars)

Fabric/Color	Size	Number
Star/red	1⅞″ x 45″	cut 1
Star/turquoise	1⅞″ x 45″	cut 1
Star/purple	1⅞″ x 45″	cut 1
Star bkgrnd./navy	1⅞″ x 45″	cut 3
Star bkgrnd./navy	1½″ x 45″	cut 2
Outside spacers/navy	1½″ x 3½″	cut 6
Inside spacers/navy	2½″ x 3½″	cut 15

MAKE STAR BLOCK UNITS

With **right** sides together, lay one 1⅞″ x 45″ strip of red fabric on top of a 1⅞″ x 45″ strip of dark blue background fabric, carefully lining up the long edges. Using the square rotary ruler, mark 12 squares (1⅞″ x 1⅞″). Draw a diagonal line through each drawn square. A strip of each fabric about 1⅞″ x 21″ should be left over after marking the squares. Save it to use for completing the star blocks. Stitch through both layers exactly ¼″ from each side of the marked diagonal line.

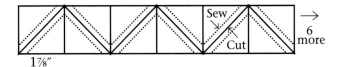

Cut on the drawn line as shown above, using the rotary square. Open the triangle and press the seam toward the dark blue fabric. Trim off points that extend beyond the squares. With the square rotary ruler, using the ruler's diagonal line, check the accuracy of the half-square triangle units; they should be 1½″ square.

Repeat steps using the turquoise fabric with the dark blue fabric and then the purple fabric with the dark blue fabric. This procedure will result in 24 half-square triangle units of each color.

Trim the remaining 1⅞″ x 21″ strips of red, turquoise, purple and dark blue to 1½″ wide strips. With the square ruler, cut six 1½″ squares each of red, turquoise, and purple for the centers of the stars. Layer the three remaining dark blue strips and cut into 1½″ squares. Use the 1½″ x 45″ strips to finish cutting a total of 72 dark blue background squares.

ASSEMBLE STAR BLOCKS

Lay out one red star block and chain-stitch in vertical rows as shown. Repeat for the other red star blocks and the turquoise and purple star blocks.

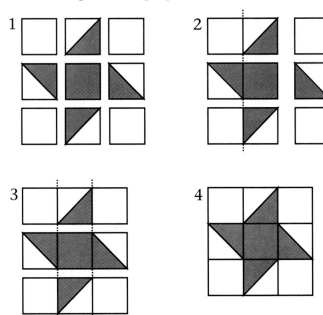

ASSEMBLE THREE ROWS OF STAR BLOCKS

Each row of stars consists of six stars of three different fabrics with a 2½″ x 3½″rectangle of dark blue background fabric between stars. The first and last rectangles are 1½″ x 3½″. To complete each row, sew a tan sashing strip 1½″ x 30½″ to the top and bottom of each row of stars.

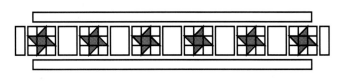

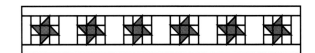

ASSEMBLE ROWS

Stitch blocks together in rows as shown in the *Quilt Top Assembly Diagram* on page 100. Next, sew the rows together. The inside unit of the quilt should now measure 30½" x 57½". Stitch a 1½" x 57½" tan background strip to each side of the quilt. (See *Preliminary Cutting* on page 51.) Sew the 4½" x 57½" red tent fabric strips to sides of quilt. Assemble the tent top and sky by stitching a sky triangle to each side of the tent top triangle as shown. This unit should now measure 40½" x 12½".

MAKE TENT SCALLOPS

Make 8 red tent scallops as instructed in the *Loose Inserts* section of the *General Directions*. Pattern on page 123. Pin scallops, matching the raw edges of the top of the scallop to the raw edge of the pieced block unit. Be careful to place the two end scallops ¼" in from the sides of the quilt so they are not caught in the seam when you add the outside borders. With **right** sides together, line up edges of the tent top unit with the edge of the pieced block unit and stitch through all layers. The scallops will be sandwiched in between these pieces. Press the seams toward the tent top.

ATTACH BORDERS AND BACKING

Stitch the blue outside borders, starting with the right and left sides. Then add the bottom and top borders. Press these seams toward the borders. Stitch the backing horizontally, referring to *General Directions, Finishing*.

FINISH

See *General Directions* for layering, basting, quilting, and binding suggestions.

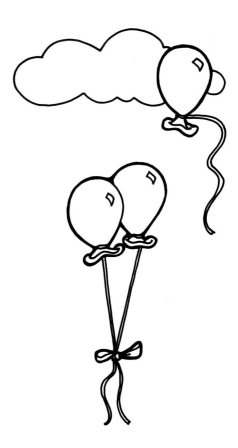

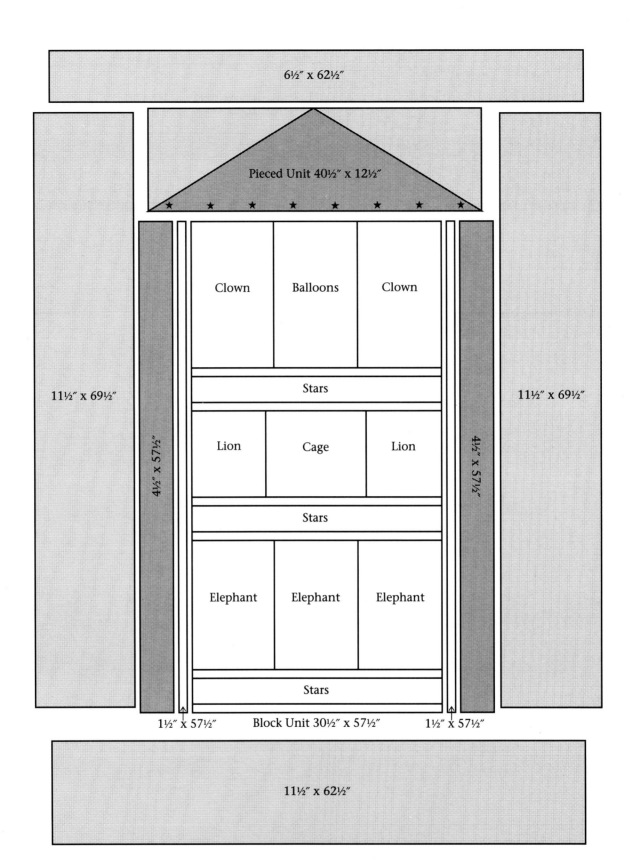

6½" x 62½"

Pieced Unit 40½" x 12½"

11½" x 69½"

11½" x 69½"

4½" x 57½"

4½" x 57½"

Clown	Balloons	Clown

Stars

Lion	Cage	Lion

Stars

Elephant	Elephant	Elephant

Stars

1½" x 57½" Block Unit 30½" x 57½" 1½" x 57½"

11½" x 62½"

UNDER THE BIG TOP
QUILT TOP ASSEMBLY DIAGRAM
Dimensions include seam allowance.

STUDENT'S DESK
Finished Size 11" x 23"

CUT

Fabric/Color	Pieces	Size or #
Background/ cream print #2	#8, 9	3" x 8"
	#10	11½" x 5"
	#11	1½" x 4½"
	#12	6½" x 3"
	#15	2" x 1½"
	#16	3" x 4½"
	#17	2½" x 5½"
	#19	3½" x 5½"
	#20	4" x 1½"
	#22	3½" x 1½"
	#24	3½" x 2"
	#27	1½" x 9½"
	#28	11½" x 2½"
Desk/solid purple	#13	6½" x 1"
	#17a, 19a	1½" x 1½"
	#18	1½" x 5½"
Drawer/med. purple	#14	5" x 1½"
	#15a	1½" x 1½"
Chair/gold print	#21	4" x 1½"
	#23	3½" x 1"
	#25	1" x 3½"
	#26	1" x 9½"
Portrait bkgrnd./ tan print	#1	6½" x 8"

Applique Pieces (patterns on page 130)

Shirt/freezer paper	#2	trace 1
Coat/freezer paper	#3, 4	trace 1
Hair/freezer paper	#5, 7	trace 1
Face/freezer paper	#6	trace 1

APPLIQUE

Applique portrait in numerical order to #1 before piecing block. Do not turn under straight edges on #2; it will be sewn into bottom and side seams when block is constructed. Refer to *General Directions, Applique*.

PIECE

Assemble block in units following diagram. Review construction of Fast Forty-Fives in *General Directions* (1a, 1b, etc.).

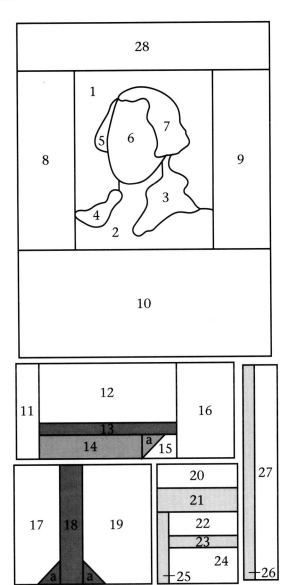

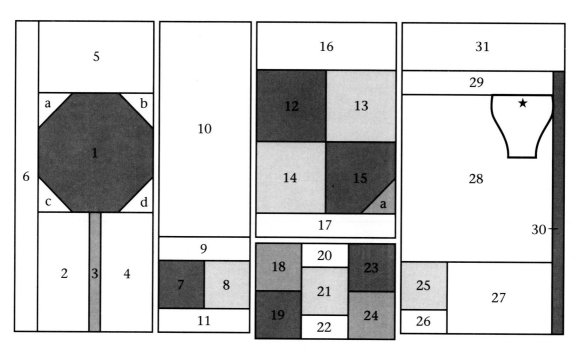

CUT

Fabric/Color	Pieces	Size or #
Background/ cream print #3	#1a, 1b, 1c, 1d	2″ x 2″
	#2, 4	2¾″ x 5½″
	#5	5½″ x 3½″
	#6	1½″ x 13½″
	#9, 11	4½″ x 1½″
	#10	4½″ x 9½″
	#16	6½″ x 2½″
	#17	6½″ x 1½″
	#20, 22, 26	2½″ x 1½″
	#27	5″ x 3½″
	#28	7″ x 7½″
	#29	7″ x 1½″
	#31	7½″ x 2½″
Stop sign, four square/hot pink	#1	5½″ x 5½″
	#15a	2″ x 2″
Posts/speckled black	#3	1″ x 5½″
	#30	1″ x 11½″
Four square/purple	#12, 15	3½″ x 3½″
Four square/turquoise	#13, 14	3½″ x 3½″
Hopscotch/8 colors	#7, 8, 18, 19, 21, 23, 24, 25	2½″ x 2½″
Loose Insert (pattern on page 125)		
Hoop/freezer paper	hoop	trace 1

PIECE

Make basketball hoop, referring to loose inserts section of *General Directions*. Assemble block in units following diagram, stitching basketball hoop into seam indicated by star on diagram. Review construction of Fast Forty-Fives in *General Directions* (1a, 1b, etc.).

SWINGSET
Finished Size 24″ x 13″

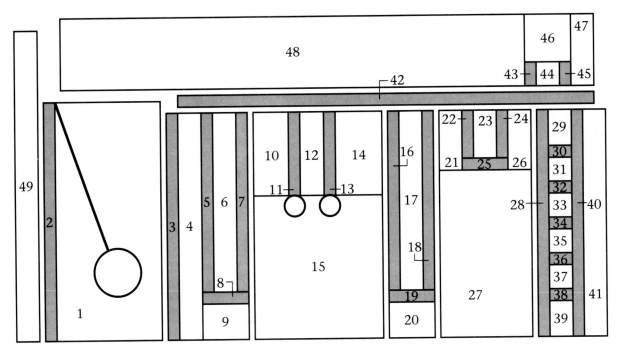

CUT

Fabric/Color	Pieces	Size or #
Background/ cream print #3	#1	5″ x 10½″
	#4, 41	1½″ x 10″
	#6, 17	1½″ x 8″
	#9, 20	2½″ x 2″
	#10	2″ x 4″
	#12	1½″ x 4″
	#14	2½″ x 4″
	#15	6″ x 6½″
	#21, 26	1½″ x 3″
	#23	1½″ x 2½″
	#27	4½″ x 7½″
	#31, 33, 35, 37, 44	1½″ x 1½″
	#29, 39	1½″ x 2″
	#46	2½″ x 2½″
	#47	1½″ x 3½″
	#48	20½″ x 3½″
	#49	1½″ x 13½″
Swingset/speckled black	#2	1″ x 10½″
	#3, 28, 40	1″ x 10″
	#5, 7, 16, 18	1″ x 8″
	#8, 19, 25	2½″ x 1″
	#11, 13	1″ x 4″
	#22, 24	1″ x 2½″
	#30, 32, 34, 36, 38	1½″ x 1″
	#42	18½″ x 1″
	#43, 45	1″ x 1½″

Applique Pieces (patterns on page 134)

Rings/cardboard	1″ circle	cut 1
Tether rope/¼″ ribbon	7″	cut 1
Tether ball/cardboard	2″ circle	cut 1

PIECE

Assemble block in units following diagram. Review accurate ¼″ seams in *General Directions*.

APPLIQUE

Review *General Directions, Applique* for preparing circles. Applique two rings and tether ball.

ASSEMBLE ROWS

Sew blocks together as shown in the *Quilt Assembly Diagram*. This unit should measure 47½" x 55½".

CUT & ATTACH BORDERS

Cut black print border:
    Two strips 5" x 55½"
    Two strips 5" x 56½"
Stitch the 55½" borders to the sides of the quilt, and the 56½" borders to the top and bottom.

FINISH

See *General Directions* for layering, basting, quilting, and binding suggestions.

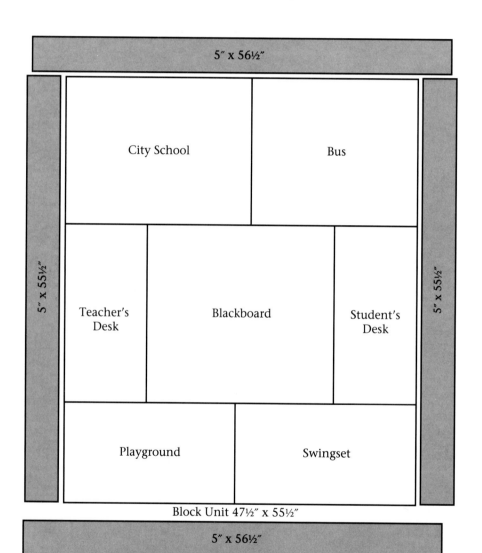

READING, 'RITING, & RECESS
QUILT TOP ASSEMBLY DIAGRAM
Dimensions include seam allowance.

SEAL
Finished Size 6″ x 7″

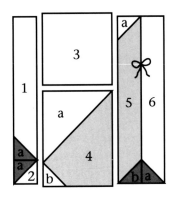

For ease of piecing, the seal block has been simplified from the original quilt. See page 64 for photo of simplified seal made into a wallhanging.

Cutting chart is for one block only. **Make four blocks.**

CUT (*cut first)

Fabric/Color	Piece or #	Size or #
Bkgrnd./tan	*cut 1	24½″ x 2½″
Bkgrnd./tan (blocks)	#1	1½″ x 6½″
	#2, 4b, 5a	1½″ x 1½″
	#3, 4a	3½″ x 3½″
	#6	1½″ x 7½″
Body/blue	#4	3½″ x 4½″
	#5	1½″ x 7½″
Front flippers & tail/dk. blue	#1a, 2a, 5b, 6a	1½″ x 1½″
Applique Piece (pattern on page 134)		
Balls/cardboard	1⅞″ circle	cut 1
Ribbons/¼″ grosgrain	6″	cut 1

PIECE
Assemble four blocks in units following diagram. Review construction of Fast Forty-Fives (1a, 1b, etc.) in *General Directions*.

ASSEMBLE ROW
Sew the four seal blocks together. Stitch the 24½″ x 2½″ background strip to the top of the row.

APPLIQUE
Applique a ball on the tip of each seal's nose. See *General Directions, Applique* for preparing circles. Hand stitch ribbon bows to seals' necks.

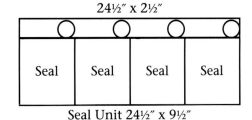

24½″ x 2½″

Seal Unit 24½″ x 9½″

SEAL WALLHANGING - 30″ x 18″
Sew four seal blocks side by side. Stitch a 24½″ x 3½″ background strip to the top of the row. Applique a ball above each seal's nose, referring to photo on page 64 for placement. Add a 3″ border.

105

ASSEMBLE BLOCKS

Fabric measurements are based on cutting from selvage to selvage. Therefore, one way designs should be avoided.

Cut: two strips 2½″ x 36½″
     two strips 2½″ x 28½″
     one strip 2½″ x 25½″
     one strip 2½″ x 24½″
     one strip 2½″ x 10½″
     two strips 2½″ x 12½″
     one strip 2½″ x 6½″

Sew sashing strips and blocks together as shown.

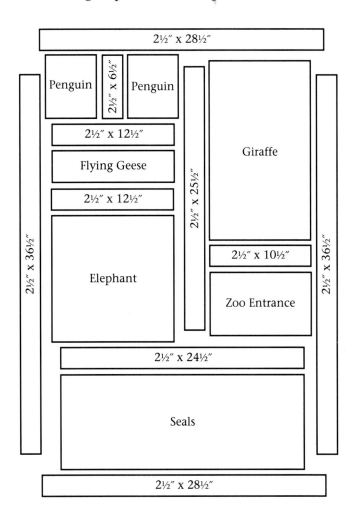

CUT & SEW RAIL FENCE BORDER

Finished block size 4″ x 4″
Cut: five blue strips 1½″ x 45″
     five gold strips 1½″ x 45″
     five green strips 1½″ x 45″
     five red strips 1½″ x 45″

Sew five sets of strips as shown. Cut nine 4½″ rail fence blocks from each strip set for a total of 45.

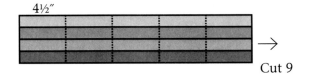

Sew 38 rail fence blocks into borders as illustrated. Note that top and bottom borders are not alike. Stitch side borders to quilt first, then top and bottom, referring to *Quilt Top Assembly Diagram*.

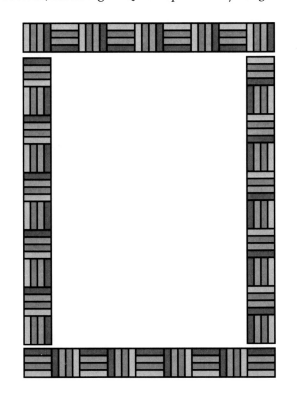

MAKE HANGERS

Use five rail fence blocks to make hangers. Cut five pieces of fabric from your stash 4½″ x 4½″ to use as backing for the hangers. Lay block and backing piece right sides together and stitch opposite edges. Turn. Fold in half and pin raw edges together. Match to vertical rail fence blocks at top edge of quilt, referring to whole quilt diagram; baste in place on the back side so the hangers will be caught in the seam when attaching binding strip.

FINISH

See *General Directions* for layering, basting, quilting, and binding suggestions.

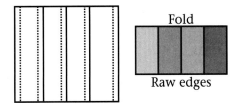

Fold

Raw edges

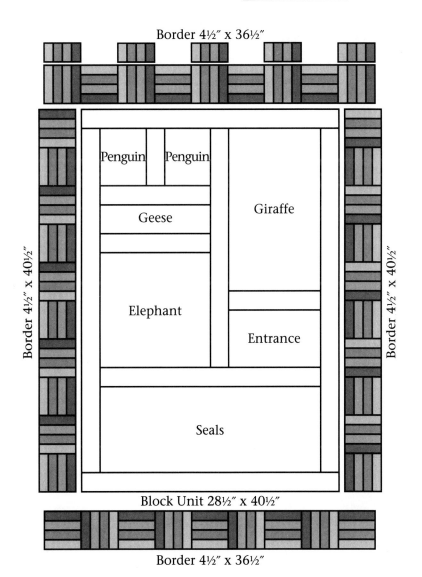

Border 4½″ x 36½″

Penguin　Penguin

Geese

Giraffe

Elephant

Entrance

Seals

Border 4½″ x 40½″

Border 4½″ x 40½″

Block Unit 28½″ x 40½″

Border 4½″ x 36½″

TRIP TO THE ZOO
QUILT TOP ASSEMBLY DIAGRAM
Dimensions include seam allowance.

HOUSE - TREE
Finished Size 16″ x 13½″

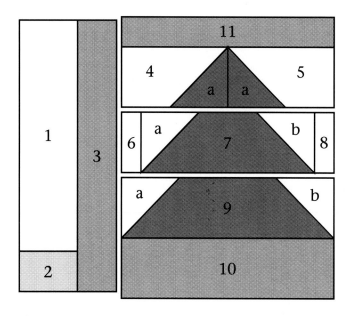

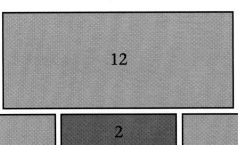

CUT

Fabric/Color	Pieces	Size or #
Background/navy stars	#1	3½″ x 12″
House/red plaid	#3	2½″ x 14″
	#10	11½″ x 3½″
	#11	11½″ x 2″
Tree/3 greens	#4a, 5a	3½″ x 3½″
	#7	9½″ x 3½″
	#9	11½″ x 3½″
Window/bkgrnd. tan	#4, 5	6″ x 3½″
	#6, 8	1½″ x 3½″
	#7a, 7b, 9a, 9b	3½″ x 3½″
Snow/white	#2	3½″ x 2½″

PIECE
Assemble block in units following diagram. Review construction of Fast Forty-Fives in *General Directions* (1a, 1b, etc.). Optional: Sew on buttons or charms to decorate the tree.

HOUSE - DOOR
Finished Size 10″ x 13½″

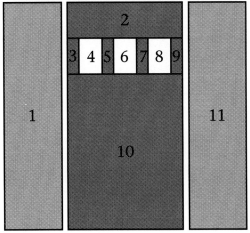

CUT

Fabric/Color	Pieces	Size or #
Door/blue check	#2	5½″ x 2″
	#3, 5, 7, 9	1″ x 2″
	#10	5½″ x 7″
House/red plaid	#1, 11	3″ x 10″
	#12	10½″ x 4½″
Windows/tan	#4, 6, 8	1½″ x 2″
Applique Piece (pattern on page 133)		
Stepping stone/freezer paper	#13	trace 3

PIECE
Assemble block in units following diagram. Review construction of Fast Forty-Fives in *General Directions* (1a, 1b, etc.). Window decorations are optional.

APPLIQUE
Wait to applique the three stepping stones, #13, until after the central block unit is assembled (see *Quilt Top Assembly*, page 110).

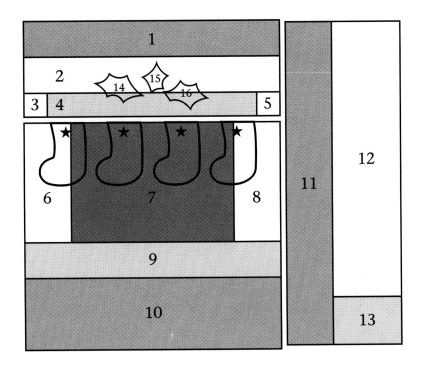

CUT

Fabric/Color	Pieces	Size or #
Background/navy stars	#12	3½″ x 12″
House/red plaid	#1	11½″ x 2″
	#10	11½″ x 3½″
	#11	2½″ x 14″
Window/bkgrnd. tan	#2	11½″ x 2″
	#3, 5	1½″ x 1½″
	#6, 8	2½″ x 5½″
Fireplace/black	#7	7½″ x 5½″
Mantle & hearth/tan	#4	9½″ x 1½″
	#9	11½″ x 2″
Snow/white	#13	3½″ x 2½″

Applique Piece (patterns on page 133)
Holly leaves/freezer paper	#14, 15, 16	trace 1 each

Loose Insert (pattern on page 133)
Stockings/freezer paper	stocking	trace 4

PIECE

Make four stockings, referring to loose inserts section of *General Directions*. Assemble block in units following diagram, stitching stockings into seam indicated by stars on diagram.

APPLIQUE

Applique holly leaves on top of mantle. Stitch red bead or button on for the holly berry. Refer to *General Directions* for applique techniques.

ROW 1

Row 1, sky and top of sleigh, was assembled on page 75.

ASSEMBLE ROW 2

Cut from the navy stars for sky:

One 25½" x 4½"
One 3½" x 10"
One 2½" x 10"

Sew as shown to reindeer blocks and front of sleigh, then stitch Santa block to right of reindeer row.

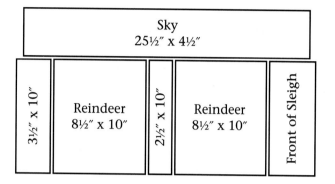

ASSEMBLE ROW 3

Sew left roof to right roof as shown in diagram in next column.

ASSEMBLE ROW 4

Sew house-tree, house-door, and house-fireplace together. See diagram in the next column.

CUT ROW 5

Cut from the white snow fabric:

One 42½" x 3½"

ASSEMBLE ROWS

Sew rows 1 through 5 together as shown.

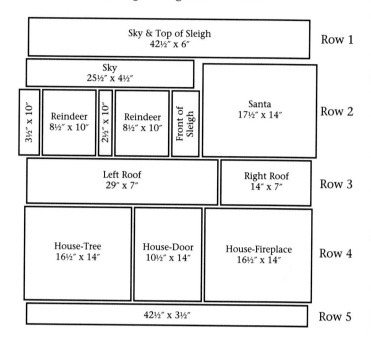

APPLIQUE

After top is assembled, applique the reindeer antlers. Applique the three stepping stones, #13, under the door.

CUT BORDERS

From the plaid inner border fabric, cut crosswise:

Two 42½" x 1"
Two 43½" x 1"

From the plaid outer border fabric, cut lengthwise:

Two 43½" x 4½"
Two 51½" x 4½"

Sew the 42½" x 1" inner borders to the top and bottom of the pieced block unit. Sew 43½" x 1" inner borders to sides of the unit. Sew 43½" x 4½" outer borders to the top and bottom. Sew 51½" x 4½" outer borders to the sides. See *Quilt Top Assembly Diagram*, page 111.

FINISH

See *General Directions* for layering, basting, quilting, and binding suggestions.

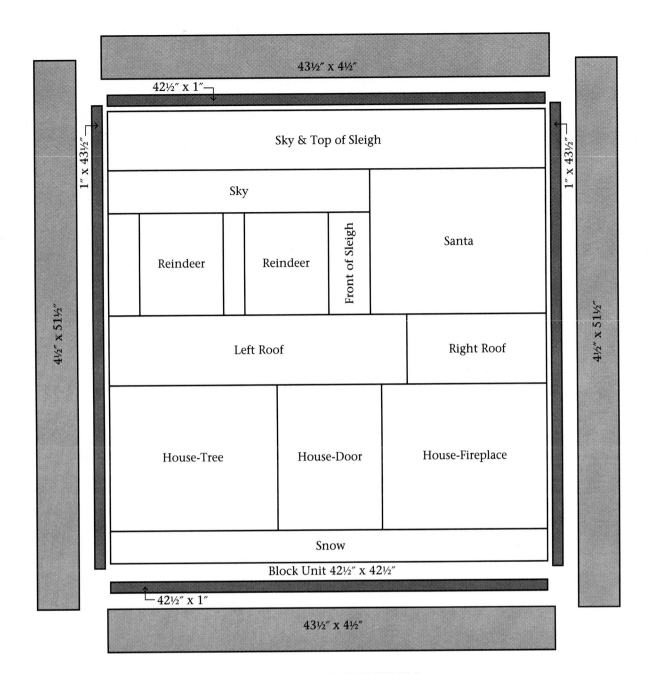

SEEING IS BELIEVING
QUILT TOP ASSEMBLY DIAGRAM
Dimensions include seam allowance.

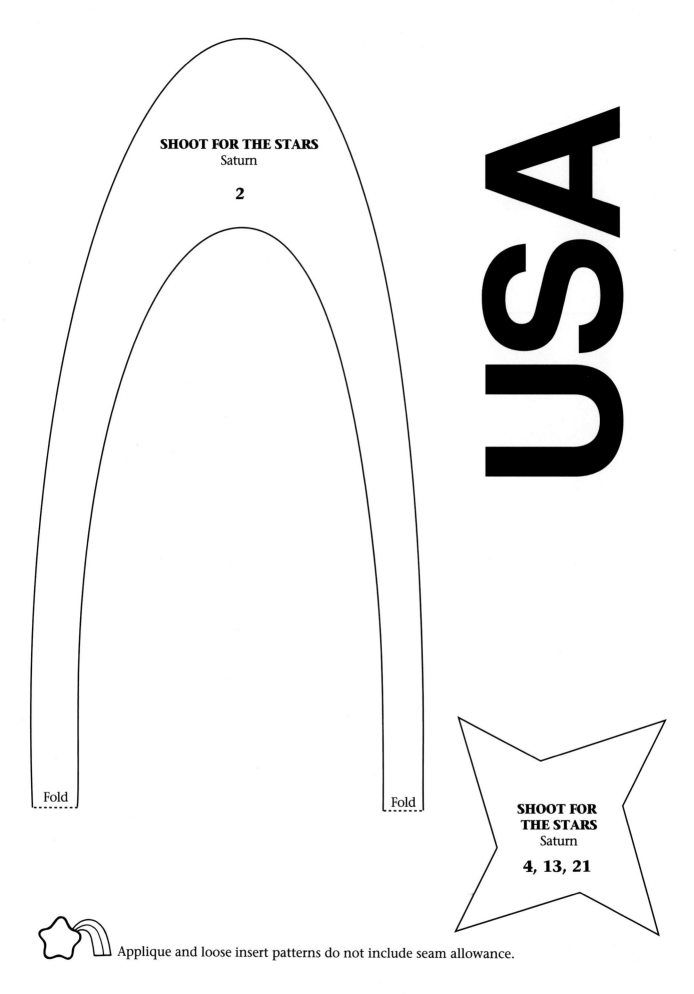

SHOOT FOR THE STARS
Saturn

2

Fold

Fold

SHOOT FOR THE STARS
Saturn

4, 13, 21

Applique and loose insert patterns do not include seam allowance.

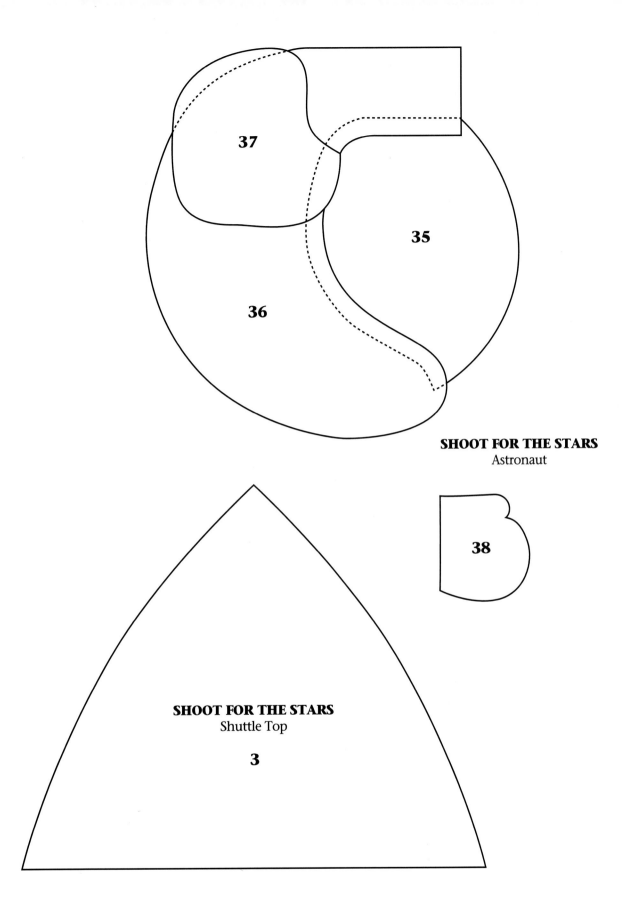

37

35

36

SHOOT FOR THE STARS
Astronaut

38

SHOOT FOR THE STARS
Shuttle Top

3

 Applique and loose insert patterns do not include seam allowance.

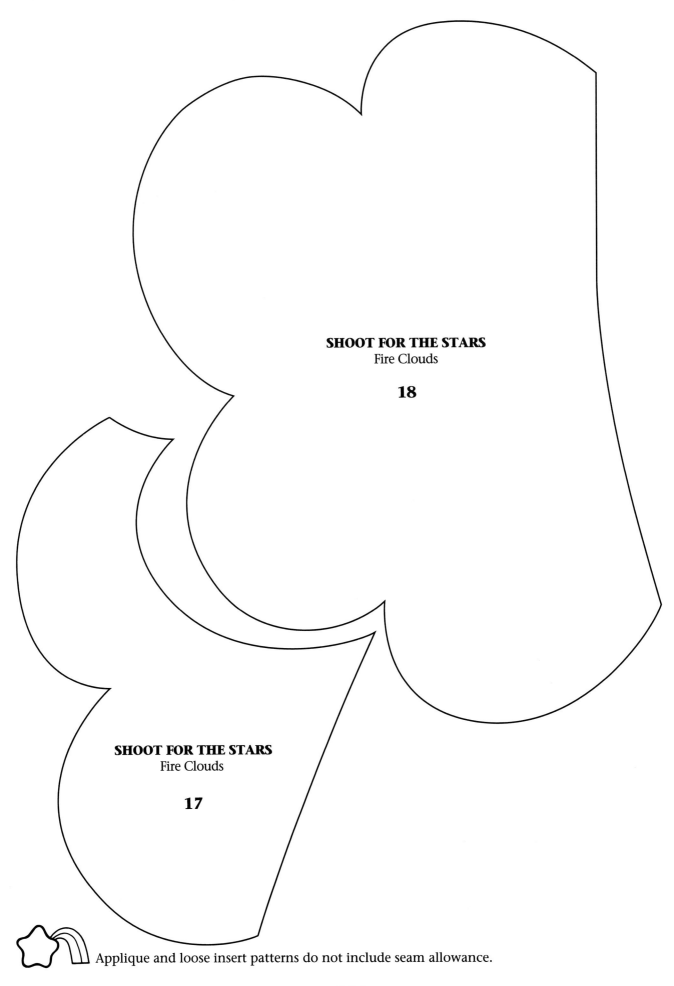

SHOOT FOR THE STARS
Fire Clouds

18

SHOOT FOR THE STARS
Fire Clouds

17

Applique and loose insert patterns do not include seam allowance.

114

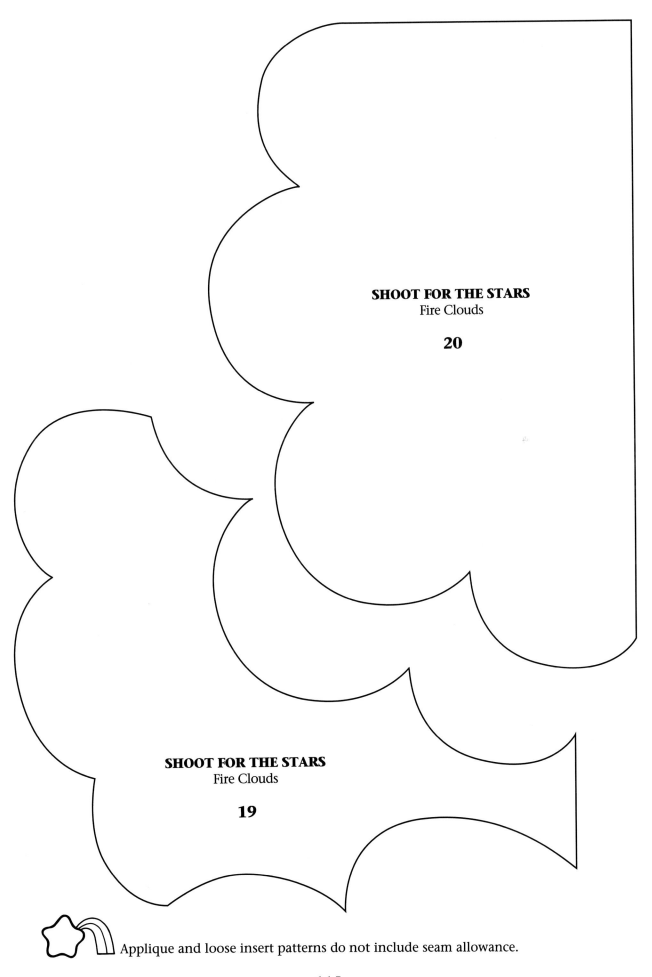

SHOOT FOR THE STARS
Fire Clouds

20

SHOOT FOR THE STARS
Fire Clouds

19

Applique and loose insert patterns do not include seam allowance.

115

Match notch to piece 22

SHOOT FOR THE STARS
Earth

21

Cut 1 from fabric after joining
pattern pieces 21 and 22

 Applique and loose insert patterns do not include seam allowance.

SHOOT FOR THE STARS
Earth

22

Cut 1 from fabric after joining
pattern pieces 21 and 22

Match notch to piece 21

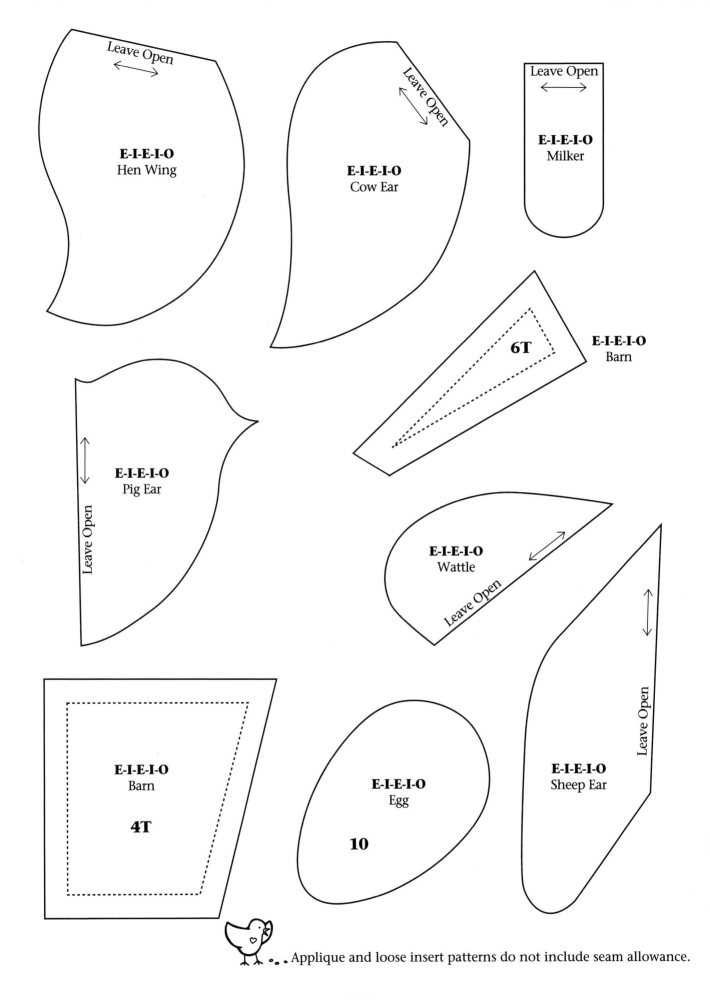

E-I-E-I-O
Hen Wing

Leave Open

E-I-E-I-O
Cow Ear

Leave Open

Leave Open

E-I-E-I-O
Milker

E-I-E-I-O
Pig Ear

Leave Open

6T

E-I-E-I-O
Barn

E-I-E-I-O
Wattle

Leave Open

Leave Open

E-I-E-I-O
Barn

4T

E-I-E-I-O
Egg

10

E-I-E-I-O
Sheep Ear

Applique and loose insert patterns do not include seam allowance.

118

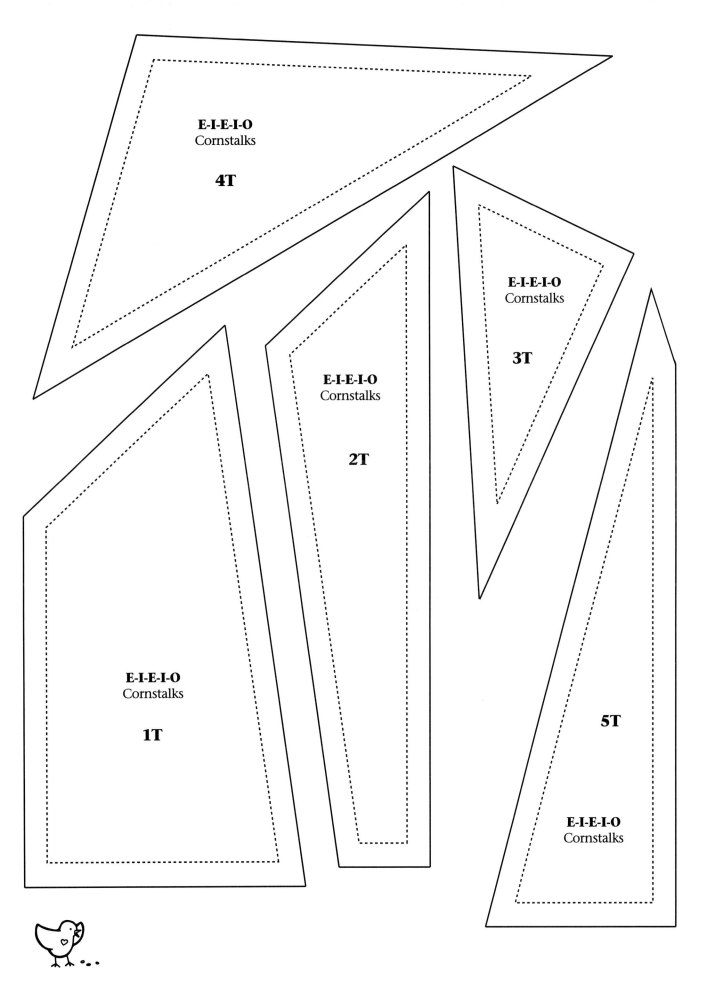

E-I-E-I-O
Cornstalks

4T

E-I-E-I-O
Cornstalks

3T

E-I-E-I-O
Cornstalks

2T

E-I-E-I-O
Cornstalks

1T

5T

E-I-E-I-O
Cornstalks

26 Fire Engine

16 Tow Truck

Emergency Lights

9 Police Car

24 Ambulance

Police Car **10**

Tow Truck Hook **15**

Y I5

Corner Blocks

STOP

WHEELS & MORE WHEELS

 Applique and loose insert patterns do not include seam allowance.

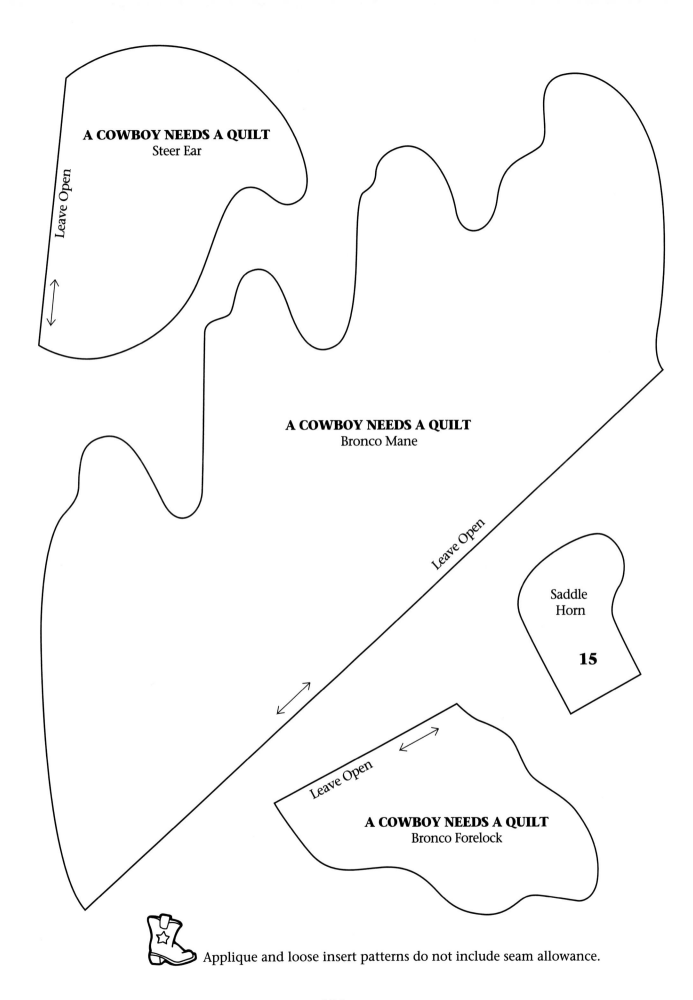

A COWBOY NEEDS A QUILT
Steer Ear

Leave Open

A COWBOY NEEDS A QUILT
Bronco Mane

Leave Open

Saddle
Horn

15

Leave Open

A COWBOY NEEDS A QUILT
Bronco Forelock

Applique and loose insert patterns do not include seam allowance.

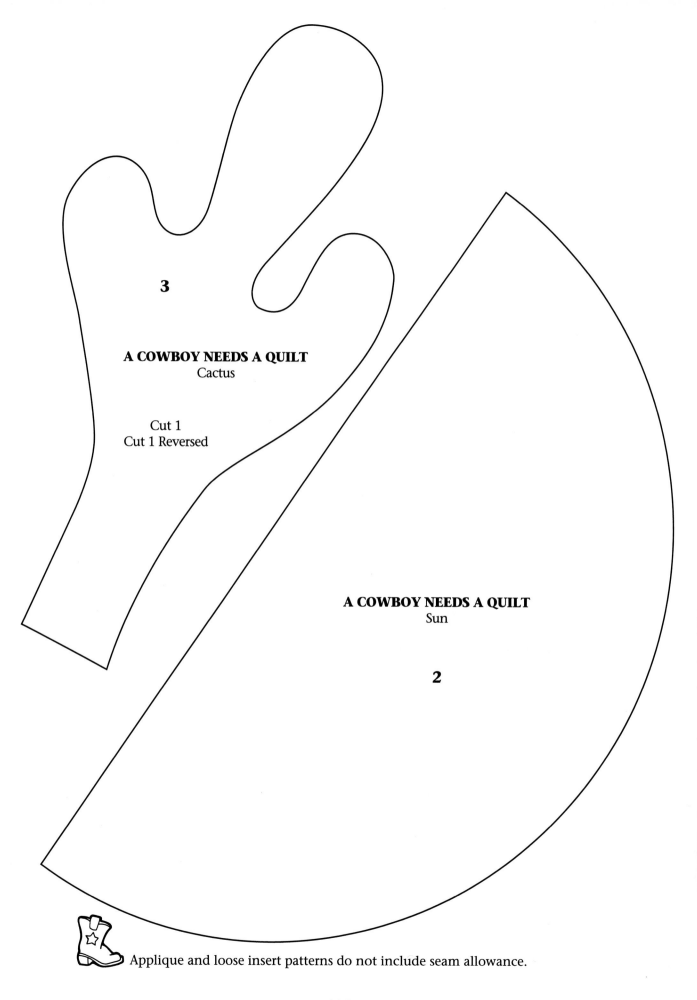

A COWBOY NEEDS A QUILT
Cactus

3

Cut 1
Cut 1 Reversed

A COWBOY NEEDS A QUILT
Sun

2

Applique and loose insert patterns do not include seam allowance.

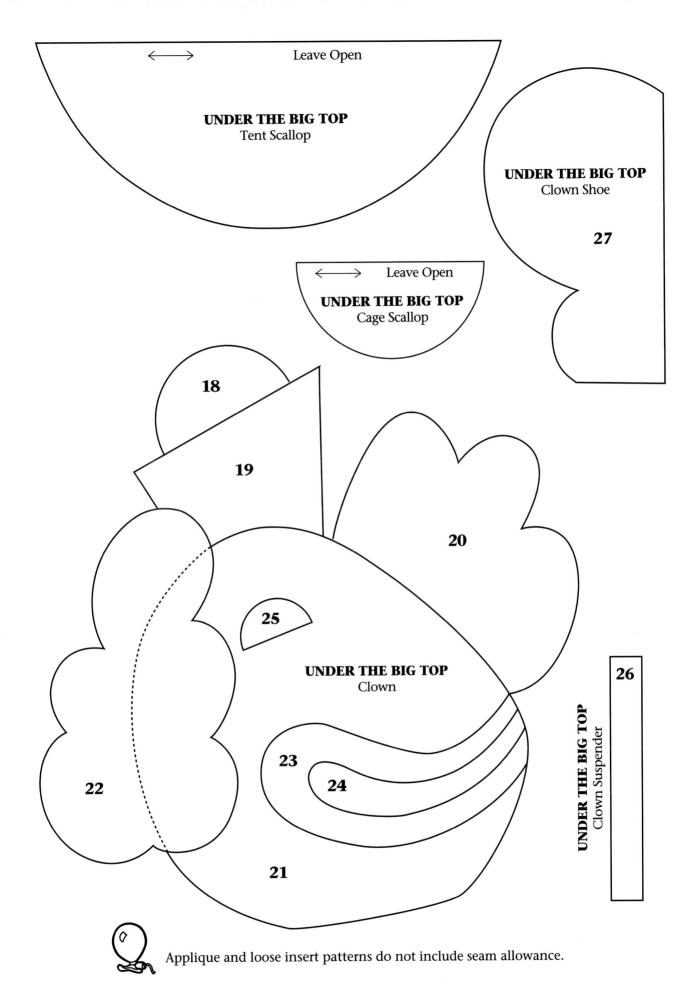

Leave Open

UNDER THE BIG TOP
Tent Scallop

UNDER THE BIG TOP
Clown Shoe

27

Leave Open

UNDER THE BIG TOP
Cage Scallop

18

19

20

25

UNDER THE BIG TOP
Clown

26

UNDER THE BIG TOP
Clown Suspender

23

24

22

21

Applique and loose insert patterns do not include seam allowance.

123

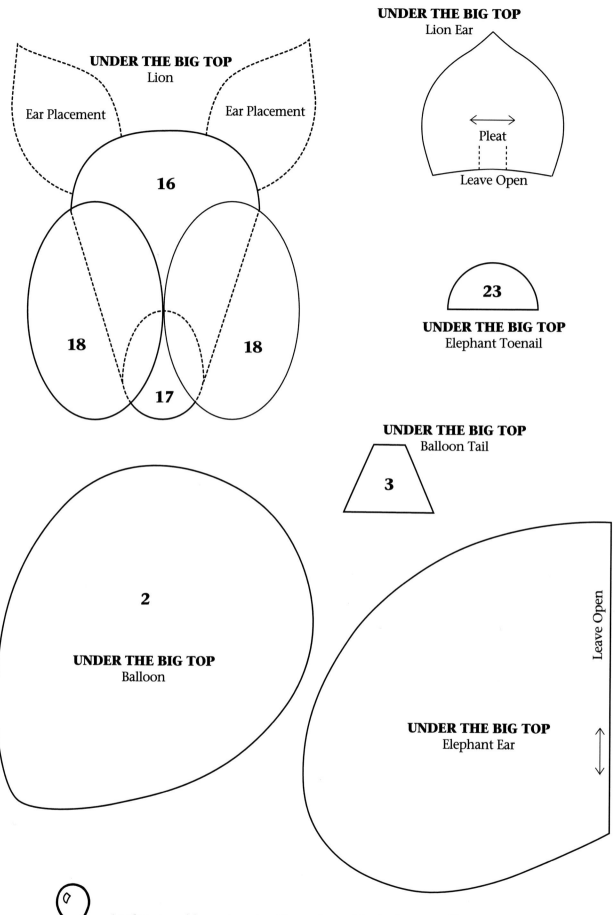

UNDER THE BIG TOP
Lion

Ear Placement   Ear Placement

16

18   18

17

UNDER THE BIG TOP
Lion Ear

Pleat

Leave Open

23

UNDER THE BIG TOP
Elephant Toenail

UNDER THE BIG TOP
Balloon Tail

3

2

UNDER THE BIG TOP
Balloon

Leave Open

UNDER THE BIG TOP
Elephant Ear

Applique and loose insert patterns do not include seam allowance.

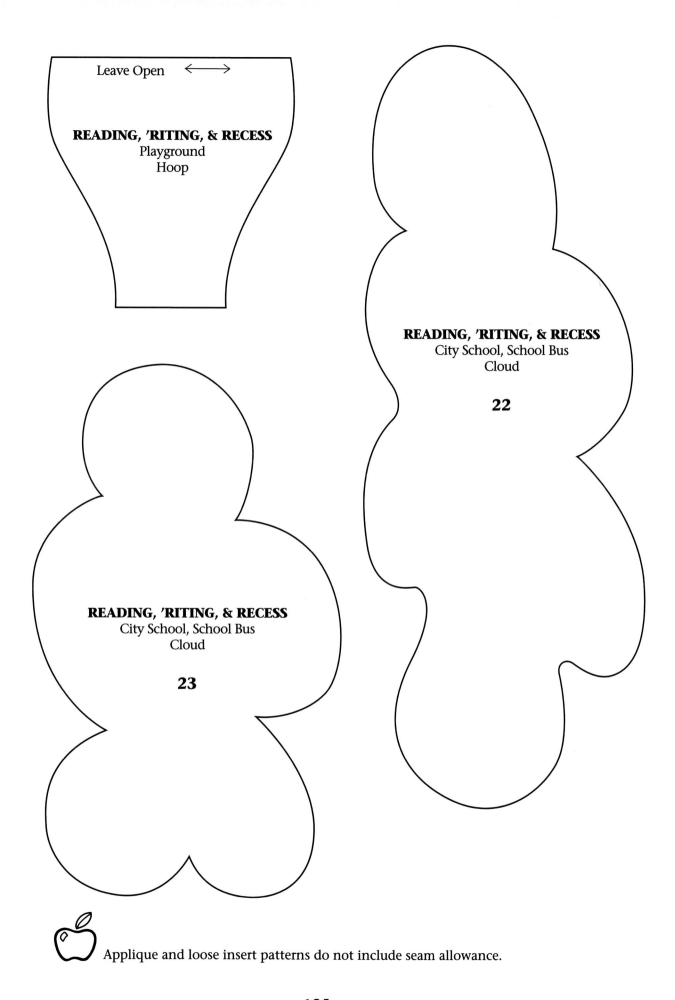

Leave Open ⟷

READING, 'RITING, & RECESS
Playground
Hoop

READING, 'RITING, & RECESS
City School, School Bus
Cloud

22

READING, 'RITING, & RECESS
City School, School Bus
Cloud

23

Applique and loose insert patterns do not include seam allowance.

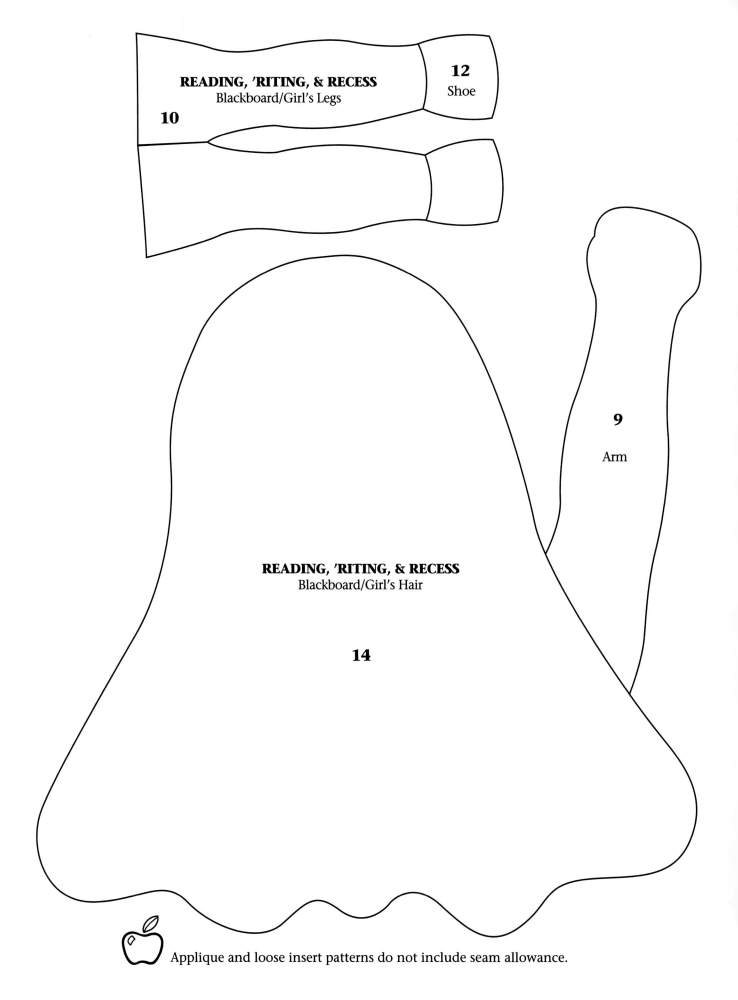

READING, 'RITING, & RECESS
Blackboard/Girl's Legs

10

12
Shoe

9

Arm

READING, 'RITING, & RECESS
Blackboard/Girl's Hair

14

Applique and loose insert patterns do not include seam allowance.

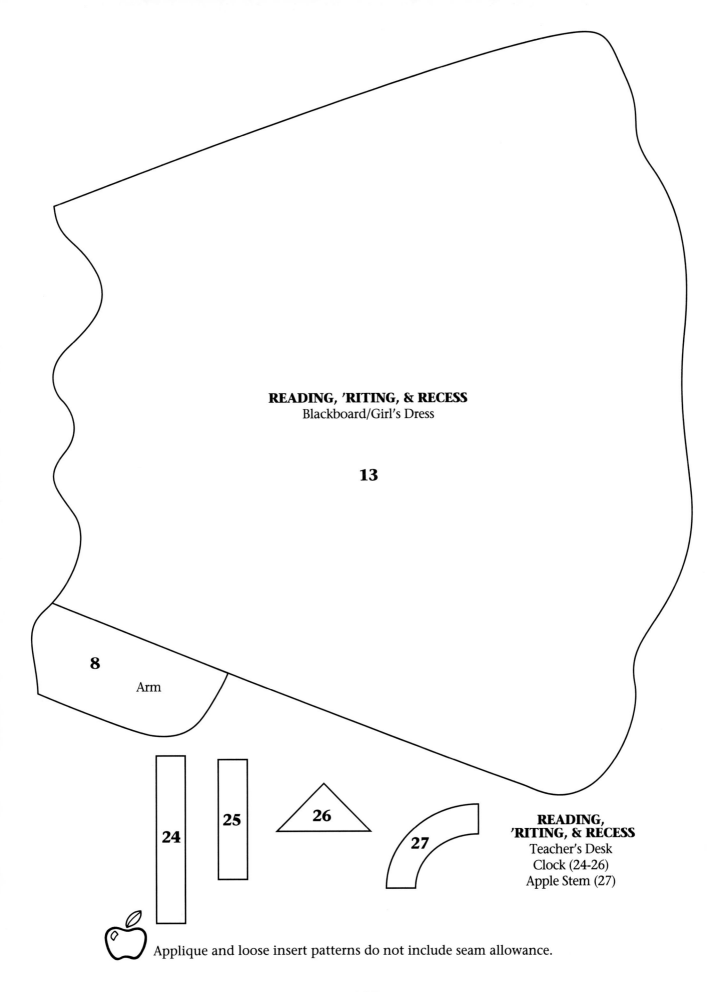

READING, 'RITING, & RECESS
Blackboard/Girl's Dress

13

8

Arm

24

25

26

27

**READING,
'RITING, & RECESS**
Teacher's Desk
Clock (24-26)
Apple Stem (27)

Applique and loose insert patterns do not include seam allowance.

127

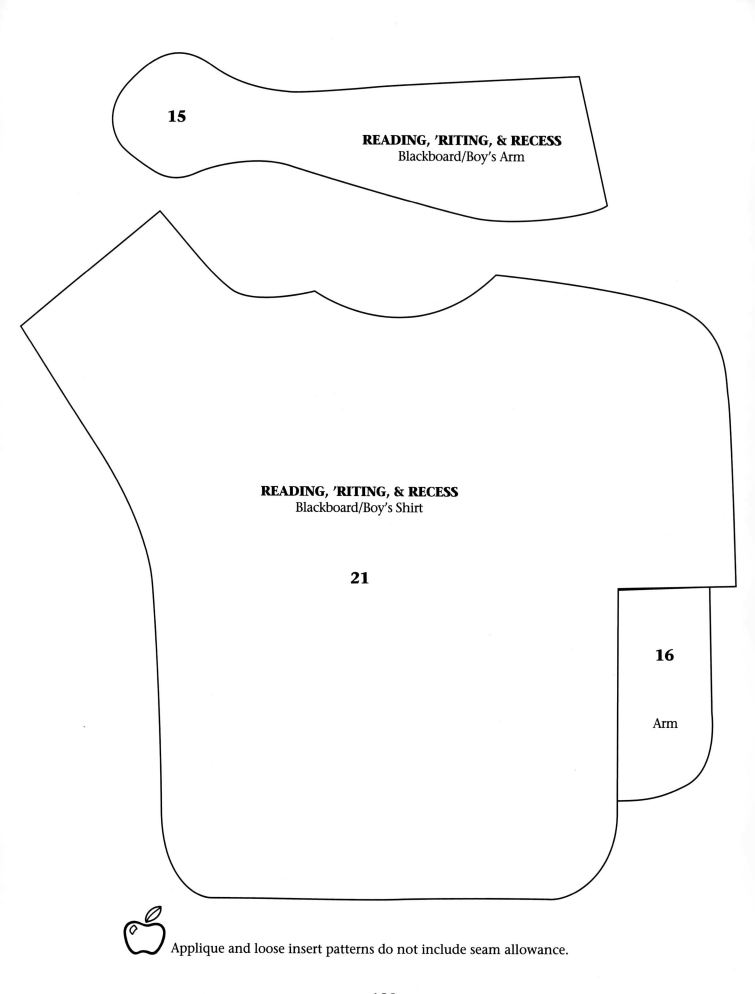

15

READING, 'RITING, & RECESS
Blackboard/Boy's Arm

READING, 'RITING, & RECESS
Blackboard/Boy's Shirt

21

16

Arm

Applique and loose insert patterns do not include seam allowance.

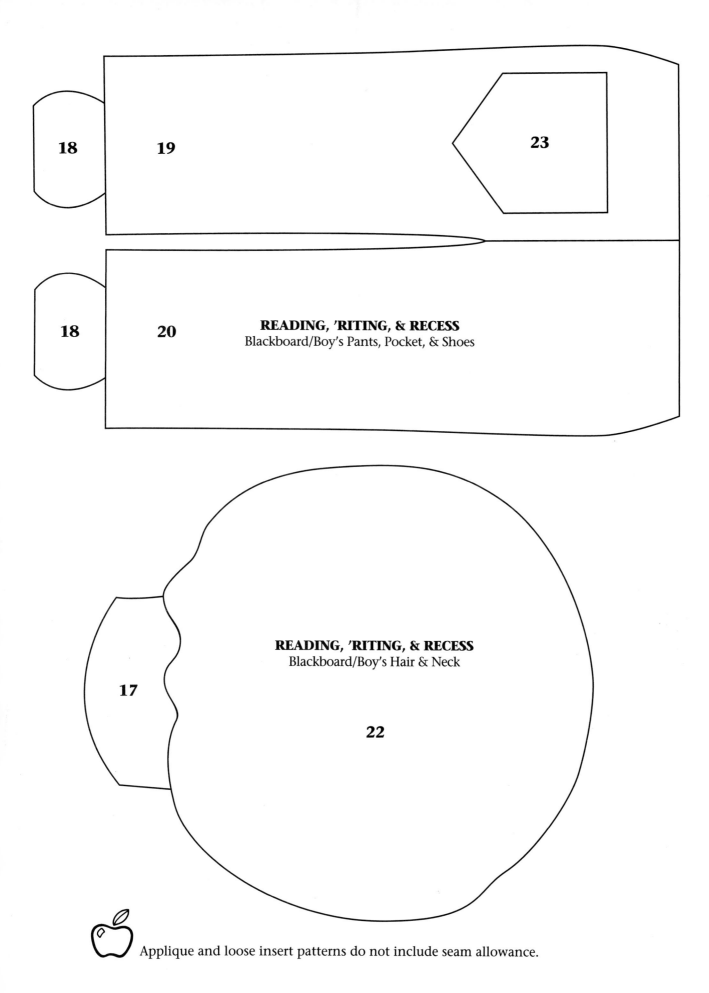

18

19

23

18

20

READING, 'RITING, & RECESS
Blackboard/Boy's Pants, Pocket, & Shoes

17

READING, 'RITING, & RECESS
Blackboard/Boy's Hair & Neck

22

Applique and loose insert patterns do not include seam allowance.

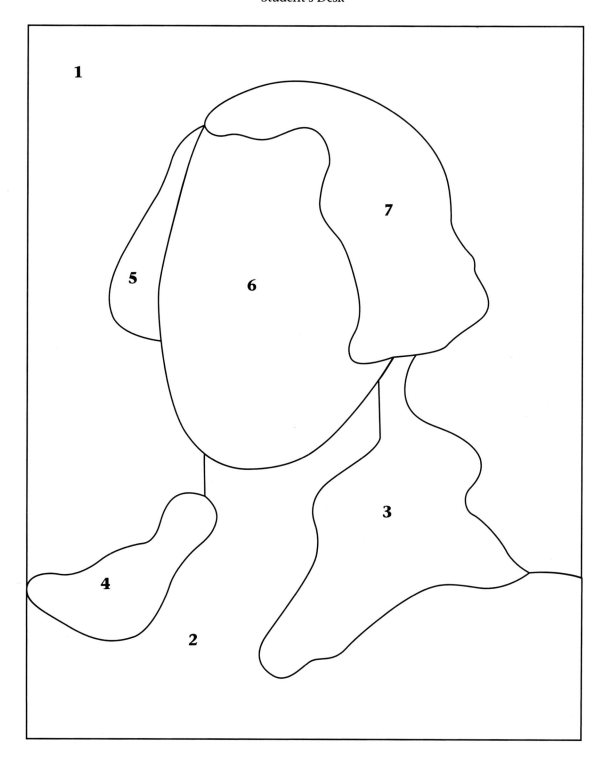

Applique and loose insert patterns do not include seam allowance.

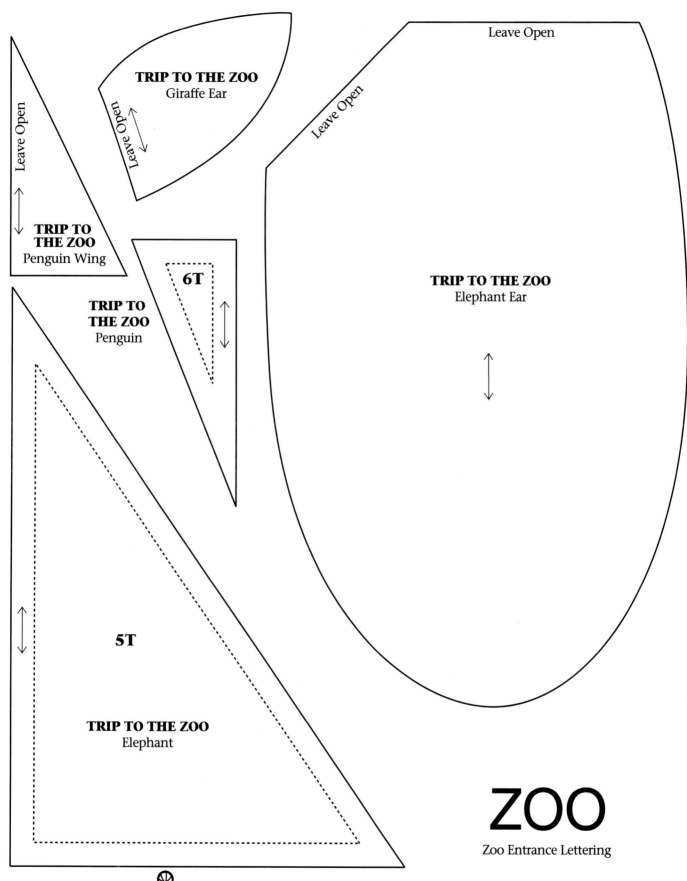

Leave Open

TRIP TO THE ZOO
Giraffe Ear

Leave Open

Leave Open

Leave Open

TRIP TO THE ZOO
Penguin Wing

TRIP TO THE ZOO
Penguin

6T

TRIP TO THE ZOO
Elephant Ear

5T

TRIP TO THE ZOO
Elephant

ZOO

Zoo Entrance Lettering

Applique and loose insert patterns do not include seam allowance.

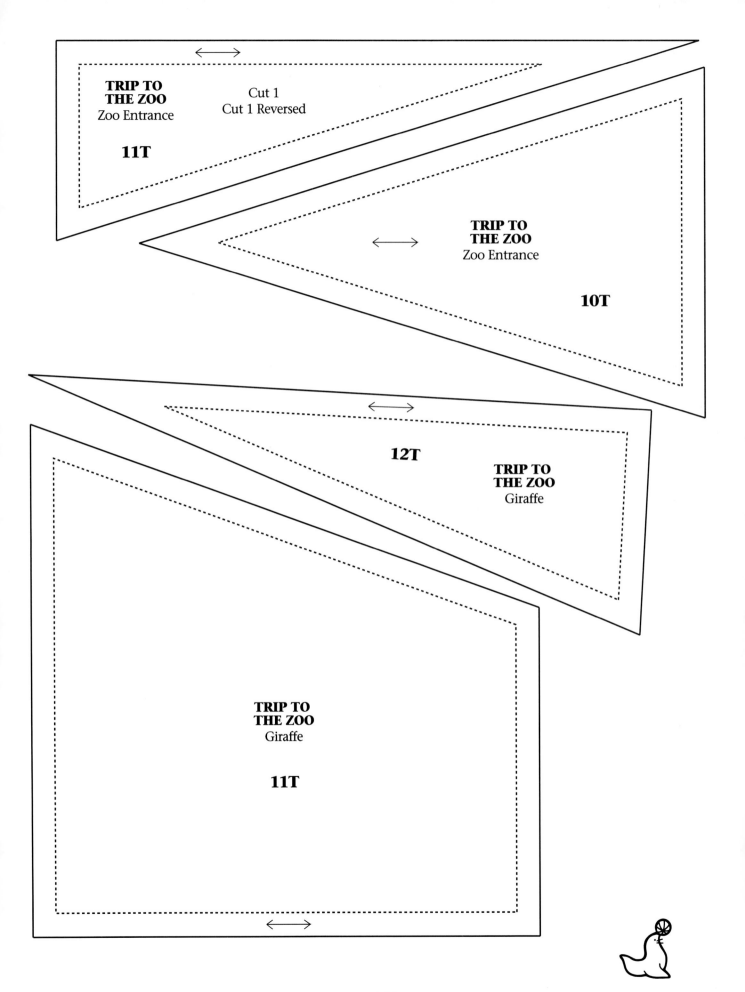

TRIP TO THE ZOO
Zoo Entrance

Cut 1
Cut 1 Reversed

11T

TRIP TO THE ZOO
Zoo Entrance

10T

12T

TRIP TO THE ZOO
Giraffe

TRIP TO THE ZOO
Giraffe

11T

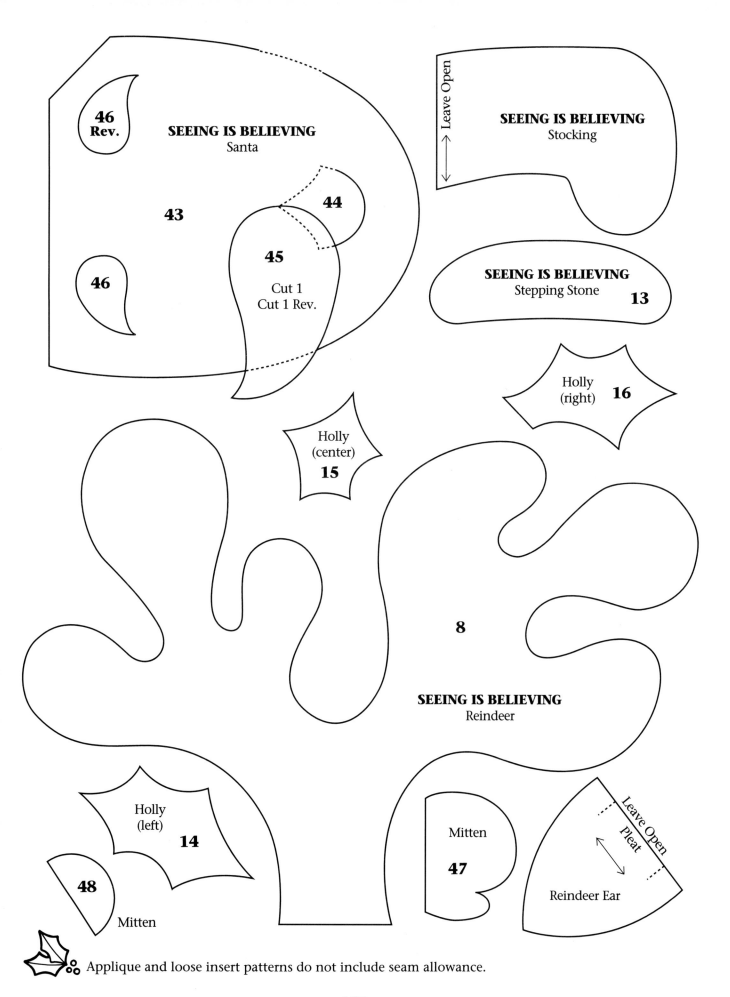

SEEING IS BELIEVING
Santa

46 Rev.

43

44

45

Cut 1
Cut 1 Rev.

46

Leave Open

SEEING IS BELIEVING
Stocking

SEEING IS BELIEVING
Stepping Stone   13

Holly
(right)   16

Holly
(center)
15

8

SEEING IS BELIEVING
Reindeer

Holly
(left)   14

48

Mitten

Mitten
47

Leave Open
Pleat

Reindeer Ear

Applique and loose insert patterns do not include seam allowance.

133

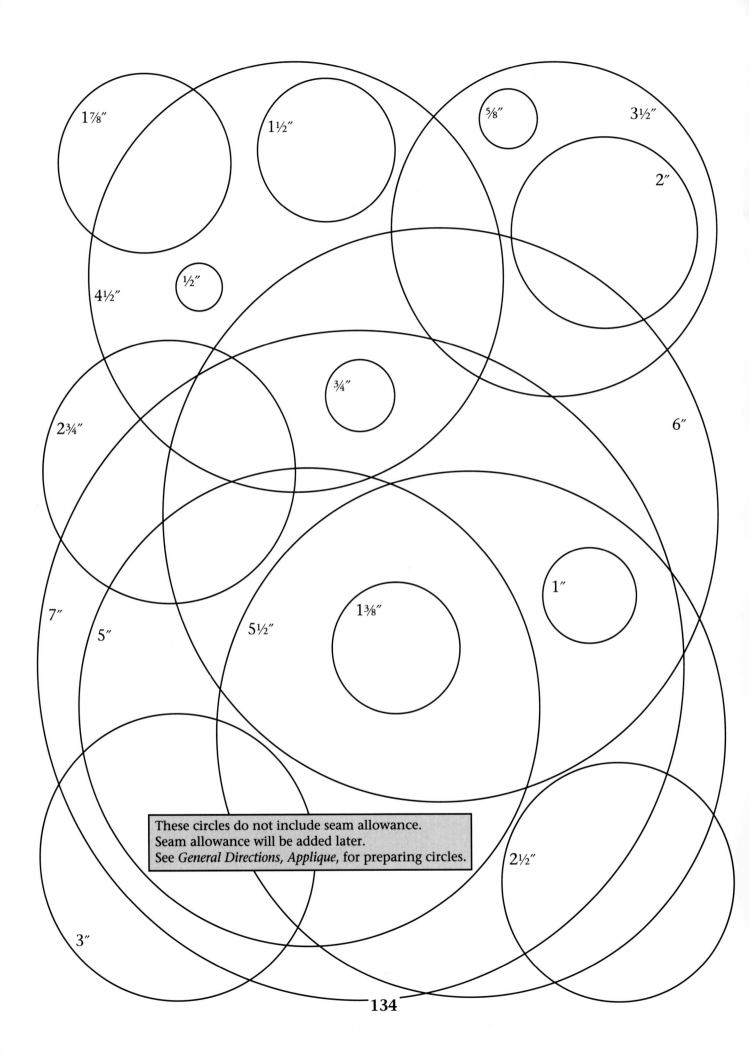

1⅞"

1½"

⅝"

3½"

2"

4½"

½"

¾"

2¾"

6"

7"

5"

5½"

1⅜"

1"

These circles do not include seam allowance.
Seam allowance will be added later.
See *General Directions, Applique,* for preparing circles.

2½"

3"

134

ABOUT THE AUTHORS

It was an adventure for Toni Phillips and Juanita Simonich to combine talents and abilities for the writing of their first book. Both are creative, energetic people whose blend of personality and talent result in a dynamic product. They encourage each other to stretch their limits.

Toni is a long-time quilt teacher and shop manager in the Denver area. During the early 1980s, she began teaching fine hand applique classes, and she soon introduced the freezer paper applique method that she adapted from stenciling. "Quilt Classics", her pattern company, was known for its beautiful traditional designs done in soft pastels. She has since broadened her interests to include machine skills and a wider palette.

Creativity has shaped Juanita's life since childhood. She has degrees in home economics education and clothing and textiles. Also trained in color and design, she has exhibited at fine art shows featuring oils, caseins, batiks, and drawings. A seamstress with experience in adult education, Juanita has a diverse background which influences each design and pattern. In 1992, Juanita, along with Laura Asbell, joined Toni as partners in her pattern company, now known as "Fabric Expressions".

Other Publications from Possibilities®
CREATIVITY FOR ALL AGES!

DS1 $15.95   DS2 $15.95

Self-directed, skill-building activities for kids 7 years and over.
It's tested! It works! 72 color pages of learning fun.

DECK THE HALLS
Quilts, wallhangings, pillows, fabric holly wreath, KIDS' PROJECTS, garland, stockings, tree skirt, everything the family needs for Christmas fun!
POS-1–64 pages–$15.95

P.S. I LOVE YOU
One of the top 10 quilting books in America. 17 quilts in cradle, crib and twin. Bumper pads, dust ruffle, accessories. Exceptional collection!
POS-3–80 pages–$16.95

QUILTS SEW QUICK
Terrific for beginning quilters, quick gifts, or fast, utility quilts. 7 quilts in 3 sizes each. Large patches for today's large print fabrics.
POS-12–28 pages–$9.95

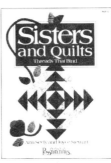

SISTERS & QUILTS
Celebration of quilts and sisterhood by award-winning quilters. 17 original quilt designs span lives of sisters, birth to "fancy free" years.
POS-13–112 pages–$19.95

ALWAYS ANGELS
Over 20 easy-to-make creative holiday projects featuring angels. Quilt, tree skirt, sweatshirt, wreath, wrapping paper, gift bag, placemats, and more!
POS-6–24 pages–$8.95

BUNCHIES
Ideas & instructions for an assortment of fast & easy Bunchies hair ornaments. Shag, flash net, sew-free, basic, fancy seams, bitsy, & others.
POS-14–24 pages–$7.95

WINDOW ZIPS
Unique memorabilia pillows with zippered vinyl pockets. Designs for baby, a family trip, a special school year, sports stars, quilters, & moving away.
POS-10–28 pages–$8.95

HOLIDAY WINDOWS
More memorabilia designs for zippered vinyl pocket pillows. Christmas, birthday, Valentine's Day, Easter, Halloween, snowman.
POS-11–28 pages–$8.95

MEMORY QUILTS
Over 15 innovative designs & ideas for planning one-of-a-kind memory quilts. Explores photos on fabric...the '90s version of memory quilts.
POS-8–104 pages–$19.95

YESTERDAY'S CHARM
Hand or contemporary applique methods let you capture both the beauty & the spirit of quiltmaking. Ten floral blocks, 4 different versions.
POS-9–20 pages–$8.95

Check with your local quilt shop.
If not available, write or call us directly.

8970 E. Hampden Ave., Denver CO 80231   303-740-6206   FAX 303-220-7424